'Xmas 94'

To Alan,
"Happy Reading"
from

U ———— x ————

GW01457979

# Speycasting

# HUGH FALKUS

## *Speycasting*

### A New Technique

"The greatest requisite in an angler is the art of throwing his line properly. Though some attain this more easily, and with less effort than others, yet it is a point which can only be gained by practice, even with the best rod; but when once learned, it is done with little comparative exertion."

JOHN YOUNGER
Shoemaker of St Boswells 1840

EXCELLENT PRESS

LONDON

First published in Great Britain 1994
by EXCELLENT PRESS 103 Lonsdale Rd,
Barnes, London SW13 9DA

Distributed in the United States of America
by Lyons & Burford, Publishers, 31 West 21 Street,
New York, NY 10010

ISBN 1 85487 331 8

A copy of the British Library Cataloguing in
Publication Data for this title is available
from the British Library

Designed by Leslie & Lorraine Gerry
Printed and bound in Great Britain by
BAS Printers Limited, Over Wallop, Hampshire

By the same author

To my pupils – my teachers


"And gladly wolde he lerne,
 and gladly teche."


The Clerk of Oxford,
from *Canterbury Tales*
Geoffrey Chaucer (c.1387)

# ACKNOWLEDGEMENTS

MANY friends deserve my thanks for their help in the preparation of this book. All have been so generous with their time that any attempt at listing them in terms of appreciation would be invidious. Perhaps an alphabetical order would seem more appropriate, but since any mention of "order" implies some form of metaphysical intervention (when none, I think, exists), better perhaps to employ the principle of *dis*order, or chaos, whence names materialise at random.

For their inimitable contributions to the text I must thank Ken Huggett, Fred Buller, Bill Arnold, David Burnett, Ken Walker, Peter Behan, Malcolm Greenhalgh, Anthony Desbruslais and, of course, Neil Barcock (see Chapter XVI), none the worse for his prolonged immersion in icy water illustrating so convincingly my recommended safety-drill in case of emergency.

Those erudite literary ferrets: David Beazley, Fred Buller, David Burnett, Peter Hunter and Charles Mason – wandering through the warrens of angling history – caught-up some delightful anecdotes both humourous and dramatic, whereas in addition to the important work started by Ben Blackwell, the photographic sequences from Mike Mutch, Fred Buller and, in particular, the indefatigable Tony Mottram, have proved crucial.

I have been greatly heartened by the open-mindedness of some of my American friends to whom the use of a fifteen-foot rod is totally foreign. That wizard of the single-handed rod and famous author of *The Cast* (1992), Ed Jaworowski, has twice travelled thousands of miles to study my casting and teaching methods and is now, arguably, by far the finest Spey-caster and instructor in the United States.

American literary guru Thomas Pero and angling photographic supremo, Benjamin Blackwell, can justly claim to be the originators of this work. Without their enthusiasm the book would never have been started.

Without the support of my beloved and long-suffering wife, Kathleen, it would never have been finished.

*Cragg Cottage*
*June 1994*

# CONTENTS

*The start of it all.*

In the life of every angler there has to be a beginning. This is the author's first piece of fishing tackle – which he watched his father make in August, 1921. A piece of broom handle split in two, drilled at the ends and formed into a hand-line frame with two lengths of raspberry cane.

With this tackle and a two-boom paternoster baited with rag-worm, the author hooked and landed a $1\frac{1}{2}$ lb whiting from an East Coast jetty. On that never-to-be-forgotten sunlit afternoon the seed was sown. Fishing became the lifetime passion that has led, finally, to this book.

# INTRODUCTION

I<small>T WOULD</small> come as no surprise to be told that in writing this book I am attempting the impossible. It has been said often enough, indeed I have said it myself, that Speycasting cannot be taught on paper. As Major Glen Grant wrote a hundred years ago:

> I hardly think that the cast can be written of so as to unveil the mystery from end to end.

So, why am I writing it? Video film would seem to present better opportunities. Well, the reason is because I want to leave a record of what I have been up to in the last twelve years or so and, compared with film, publishing offers a better chance of survival. Besides, for me, a well-produced book has an aesthetic pleasure I have seldom encountered in a video. It is true that I made a Speycasting video some years ago, but the more advanced techniques described in this book leave it somewhat outdated.

But what is it, you may well ask, that I think worthy of leaving to posterity?

Briefly, I believe that the all-round technique of Speycasting, which I teach today and is dependent on two completely different roll casts from the same shoulder, has not been taught before. In addition, the Contrived Loop Cast and the technique of Two-Way Fishing, which my friends and I have been using in recent years with great success, are both my inventions and so far as I know entirely original. Most important of all, however, as I try to make clear in the following chapters – in addition to the way my "Reverse" cast is made, with the right hand over the top of the head in the "Key" position – what makes my technique different from any other in the history of two-handed casting is the *positive use of the left (or bottom) hand*.

What I mean by "positive" use of the left hand (assuming, as I shall throughout the book, that we are casting off the right shoulder) is that the left wrist describes exactly the same forward movement as the right wrist as the power stroke is made. If anyone is Speycasting like this I have not heard about it, nor can I find much reference to it in the literature.

An exception is "Ephemera" (Edward Fitzgibbon) writing in *The Book of the Salmon* (1850):

> Propel your rod and line forwards with a strong, sharp fling, whose action is commenced by the *hands* and *wrists*, and terminated and completed by the muscular power from *elbow-joints to finger-tips* being called into forcible play. (My italics)

This is an interesting passage in that he seems to be using *both* forearms and wrists and *not* employing a see-saw action.

But Fitzgibbon appears to have been the proverbial voice crying in the wilderness, because no one took much notice of him.

"The left hand is not used except as a pivot," says one author. "Place the button of the rod butt on the palm of the left hand," says another. And again: "In making the cast, the impetus is given to the rod almost entirely by the right hand." And so on throughout the years to the present day. Not that a great deal has been written about Speycasting. Few of the old writers had much to say. Some devoted a paragraph or two; perhaps a couple of pages; occasionally a short chapter; but their descriptions of the technique are vague and the illustrations weird – matchstick men, mostly, almost without exception casting off the wrong leg and using a see-saw action of their arms as they propel the line forward.

And so, one of my motives for writing this book is to sort all this out. Another is to persuade salmon anglers that despite what has been written about it, Speycasting with the help of modern rod-making materials, is really very simple, and once the *basics* have been learned (that is, the roll casts on which my technique is based) is so much easier to perform than they have been led to think.

What people in general think about it I know only too well. Their sense of frustration has been expressed often enough during the past twelve years of teaching – during which time upwards of a thousand anglers have passed through my hands.

Unhappily, the huge improvement in salmon fly rods has not been accompanied by an improvement in Speycasting and instruction. With a few exceptions, the standard of teaching is reflected in the poor Speycasting (or absence of it altogether) on many rivers today. As an example: of the hundreds of anglers who cast their flies on a salmon river I fish regularly, week after week the seasons through, the only people seemingly able to Speycast can be counted on one's fingers – and most of those are former pupils of mine! When one considers how easily modern salmon fly rods can be handled compared with the rods of yesterday, such a state of affairs is ridiculous. But the chief reason is not a lack of interest in good casting, it is a lack of good casting instruction.

Don't misunderstand me. The ranks of the modern professional instructors contain some very knowledgeable anglers who are excellent fly casters. But if the stories I am told by numbers of disgruntled pupils are true, what many teachers today are lacking is *instruction on how to instruct*. All too often, it seems, there is a failure to appreciate the difference between teaching and demonstration.

A case in point is the single Spey cast, that manoeuvre most people refer to when talking about "Speycasting". [Note: As we shall see, once you have perfected the two roll casts I recommend, the *double* Spey cast – by far the easiest and safest of all fly casts – can be mastered in five minutes. The *single* Spey cast presents a completely different problem.]

By all the casting instructors I have met this is offered to pupils today as it always has been, on the lines of the traditional Spey, or "underhand throw" as it used to be called. Now, this is a very useful technique and I use it a lot in my fishing, as described in Chapter VII, but it is a cast that is very difficult if not impossible to *teach*. It can be *demonstrated* until the instructor's arms fall off, but neither he nor I nor anyone else can *teach* the beginner how hard to pull the fly from its position downstream to a position upstream that will compensate for the strength of the current and give the angler time and room to complete the cast.

With very few exceptions no angler can master this manoeuvre until he has had considerable experience and hours of practice. To demonstrate it is easy, but to teach it is another matter entirely. This is one reason why on many rivers the standards of Spey casting are as low as they are, and why comparatively few salmon fly-fishers aspire to anything other than the overhead cast. In itself, demonstration is very valuable, but it is not a substitute for teaching.

In a sense, this Introduction is a form of demonstration: it discusses what is to be described in detail in the book – we go, in other words, from the general to the particular. Similarly, a casting demonstration simply shows the pupil what it is that he or she is going to be taught, and in the case of the traditional Spey cast it cannot be taught.

It is interesting that George Kelson, who wrote at length about the "Spey system" in his book *The Salmon Fly: How to dress it and how to use it* (1895), sensed this dilemma:

> Let us now consider the question of force usually required … There is perhaps a little speculation as to how much force is applied in bringing the rod back and round … having no instrument to measure the degree of force applied in lifting the line, how am I to estimate it? … taking any one particular condition of wind and water, is the force definable? The question is, I think, to be answered in the negative. It seems to me to be purely an affair of judgement.

And so it is.

There are, of course, always the odd-balls. I have known a few well-co-ordinated people who have picked up the standard Spey cast straightaway from a demonstration, but they have been rare. Hundreds more have come to me in despair having spent years, in some cases lifetimes, trying unsuccessfully to master it, never having found anyone capable of teaching them. Nor, often enough, have their gillies been able to help them much. Many gillies Spey cast beautifully; but, when it comes to teaching, most of them fail completely.

And always for the same reason. You cannot *teach* someone how much force to apply in order to bring a fly upstream time after time to the exact spot you want it before casting across the river. To fish with effortless ease you must be able to cast with the accuracy of a machine, and to do that you must acquire a pattern of rod movement which is automatic.

To devise a Spey cast I *could* teach was the problem I set myself on retiring from film-making and broadcasting, and after considerable experiment I succeeded. The result was the Figure-of-Eight Spey cast. This *can* be taught because it depends entirely on its particular pattern of rod movement. No force is used in bringing the fly upstream. Apart from adjusting the rod angle to accommodate the wind speed it is all quite automatic. Make the correct movements as you swing the rod round upstream and it will bring the line upriver and place the fly exactly where you want it *every time*. Indeed, once this pattern of movement becomes instinctive you can cast in pitch darkness. Made with a single-handed rod, it is an indispensable cast for the sea trout night fly fisherman wading down bushy runs or from the banks of wooded pools.

Detailed instructions on how to do it are given later. Sufficient for now to say that, having devised a teachable Spey cast, what remained was to construct a Spey cast *Simulator* – which would help imprint a pupil with the exact shape of the rod movement necessary.

Despite the complexity of the constantly shifting planes involved, such an instrument – the Speycasting Simulator Mk. I – came into being, its construction made possible by the inspired skill of my old friend Bill Arnold.

In calm weather it worked wonderfully well, but its bulk proved a drawback in strong winds and it was soon followed by Mk. II. This streamlined model, which is in use today, induces exactly the same pattern of rod movement; but, having less wind resistance, can be mounted permanently at the waterside. With the help of this unique and invaluable casting aid, it is possible to teach any reasonably co-ordinated anglers to put out a workable Spey cast in under half-an-hour – always provided they have thoroughly mastered the basic roll cast on which it depends. And I can only suggest that the use of a similar "aid" might be helpful to all other Speycasting instructors.

I must emphasize that the Spey casts I teach are simply *re-directed roll casts*, and it must be understood that these are *not* made in the manner of the traditional roll cast usually taught today. They are made with the use of *both* wrists and punched out *above the water* with a tilted rod. Once a pupil can do this it is no exaggeration to say that use of the Simulator cuts the teaching time of the single Spey cast from hours to minutes.

*    *    *

On the evidence of recent years as I have observed it, many would-be Speycasters make things difficult for themselves by trying to combine learning with fishing. This is a huge mistake. If you want to learn how to cast well, then stick to learning. If you want to catch fish, then stick to fishing. Don't try, with hopeless optimism, to do both at the same time. When teaching on Speyside some years ago, I tried to protect my pupils from themselves by imposing Draconian measures: "Fishing verboten except before breakfast!" If, when trying to learn, you break this excellent rule, far more often than not you will finish up having learnt nothing and caught nothing. First things first. Go and

Figure-of-eight Speycasting Simulator, Mk I. For a time this casting aid – reminiscent of a Henry Moore sculpture – was the only one of its kind in the world. Today, it has to share that exalted position with the new streamlined Mk II.

Resting a rod butt in the starting groove and twirling it round the contour of the Simulator, teaches a pupil the exact movement necessary for making a single Spey cast from the left bank.

Once the shape of this rod movement is imprinted on an angler's memory, Speycasting is as easy as riding a bicycle.

18

The Figure-of-eight Speycasting Simulator, Mk II. As discussed later, after spending ten or fifteen minutes practising at the waterside, although they have never made such a movement before, most of my pupils can put out a tolerably good Spey cast. The resulting boost to their confidence is often expressed by a joyous shout: "I can do it !"

19

learn to cast properly. Concentrate on that alone. Then you will thoroughly enjoy trying to catch a salmon – be far better equipped to do it, but not be terribly downcast when you fail to do so.

Take my word for it. The delight in throwing a good line, especially in hostile conditions, lifts the spirit and more than compensates for failure to catch fish.

But how, in the light of my recent comments, are you to acquire this skill? Well, first of all find an instructor who is sympathetic to my methods of casting, as described in this book, and who appreciates the positive use of the bottom wrist; also, who understands the importance of being able to make all casts off the same shoulder. The ability to do this has everything in its favour. It makes almost every stretch of water fishable with the fly, which otherwise in certain adverse conditions (as explained in Chapter VI) would be impossible to cover. Also, it enables you to make the Contrived Loop – a most practical and delightfully simple cast.

When mastered in all its forms, Speycasting is beautiful to watch and intensely satisfying to perform. It is the very pinnacle of all angling skills and will provide lasting pleasure throughout those long, cold, fishless, and what might otherwise have been frustrating and miserable days. But the reasons why every intelligent angler should learn to Spey cast are by no means purely aesthetic. Compared with other methods of presenting a fly, Speycasting is by far the safest and most practical. Of all the ways of losing a salmon, a broken hook due to overhead casting is one of the most common. So too is physical injury both to yourself and to other people – usually your gillie or your boatman. Once you have mastered it, Speycasting protects your person as it protects your hook. It avoids false casting. It defeats the wind, however strong. By keeping your line in front of you and clear of trees, cliffs, rocks and bushes, it enables you to cover water impossible to fish with any other legal method of fly fishing. You will find that your delight in its mastery will lend another dimension to the old adage "There's more to fishing than catching fish".

It was chiefly to guide you towards the pleasures I have been lucky enough to enjoy during a long sporting lifetime that I wrote my books about salmon and sea trout fishing. To encourage you to experience the exhilaration (and the reward) that comes from casting a safe and beautiful line and perhaps fish difficult places you have not fished before is, mainly, my motive for writing this one.

Hugh Falkus
Cragg Cottage
1994

First find your fish. (Time spent in reconnaissance is seldom wasted.)

To an overhead caster wishing to cover salmon lying out of picture downstream above a weir, the cast presents problems – what with bridge, trees and overhanging branches. But to the Speycaster whose fly never travels behind him – the cast is relatively simple.

The loop of line that (as we shall see) is propelled forward in all our roll and Spey casts, should not be circular in shape. A round loop of line indicates that insufficient punch has been given in the power stroke and will tend to finish up in something of a heap. The correct, forceful, loop has more of an elliptical shape. The loop pictured below is what the power stroke of a roll cast should look like. And throughout this book, remember: all our Spey casts are simply re-directed roll casts.

When used for Speycasting, modern carbon fibre rods have a tendency to twist and separate at the joints, and subsequently break, if not strongly taped up. To avoid this, as described in the following chapter, Bill Arnold and I have glued most of our rod joints together to form one-piece rods.

To have a set of rods mounted ready for use is a great blessing, both for my teaching and for fishing trips. We each take two rods loaded with different types of line, everything having been prepared in advance at base.

On arrival at the river we have only to check the water height and temperature, select the appropriate tackle and get stuck straight in. A great saving of time and fiddle.

These "one-piece" rods cast sweetly and travel perfectly well on top of the motor. Over the years, we have carried our rods on the car roof for thousands of miles throughout Britain without mishap. For fishing abroad, if travelling by air, you will of course take conventional rods. But you are going to need some spare rods anyway.

# I   RODS AND LINES

It is of no importance what a rod is called so long as it will do its job, and the beginner will do well to remember that Speycasting can be a very tough job. When choosing a rod (or, better, rods – for we should *never* go salmon fishing with one rod only) it is also well to remember that there is a world of difference between summer fishing with floating lines and small flies, and winter (early spring and late autumn) fishing with high density, quick-sinking lines and big, often heavily-weighted, tubes. A rod that will perform well enough when casting the former may well collapse when attempting the latter.

For salmon fly fishing, only one quality rod is worth buying – the best you can get. It was well said by "Ephemera" (Edward Fitzgibbon) in *The Book of the Salmon* (1850): "A cheap salmon fly rod is the dearest thing one can buy."

Unfortunately it is true to say that we don't always get the best when we pay for it. It is equally true to say that we seldom get the best if we *don't* pay for it. So, when buying a salmon rod, be prepared to put your hand in your pocket. Only one choice is sensible.

Not long ago my publisher, a simple soul when divorced from his desk, arrived on the casting platform. "Look, Hugh," he said.

"This is my new rod. Fifteen foot, nice long cork grip; snake rings; takes a Number 11 line. It's just like the rods you use. Bit of a difference in the price though. What a bargain. I got it for less than a quarter the cost of one of your rods. What do you think of it?"

"It *looks* all right," I said. "But there's only one way to find out. Put a line on it and see what it'll do."

"Amazing bit of luck, really," he burbled on as I threaded the line. "Happened to come across it in the shop. They gave me a big discount. Got it specially for my holiday in Norway next month. I'm going after salmon this year, giving the sea trout a miss. Just the job, don't you think?"

"Could be," I said as I stood ready to cast. "We'll see. As you know, the test of a rod during a Spey cast is the strength of spring at the climax of the power stroke. In effect, when we make it, what we are trying to do is break the rod in half. Here we go …"

It broke in half.

There was what is known as a long, pregnant silence. Lost for words, the literary crocodile stood open-jawed.

"Well, there you are," I said, handing him back his bits and pieces. "What do you think of your great bargain now? Listen my dear fellow," I went on, sensing he was near to tears. "Don't take it to heart, it's all happened before often enough. Just return that rubbish whence it came and try to get your money back, or at least a replacement. In the meantime I'll lend you a proper rod to take to Norway."

Big-headed show-off, I don't know why he didn't push me in, but he restrained himself, took my advice and went off on the best salmon fishing holiday of his life. The 15 ft. salmon Speycaster I lent him didn't let him down and he now owns two of them.

By the way, don't think I'm trying to sell you a rod. I'm not. This book is not a sales catalogue. Besides, I would never make that mistake. Choosing a fly rod is an arcane rite. Like the choice of a gun or a motor car it is a very personal matter. However well I knew a man I would no sooner choose a rod for him than choose him a girlfriend. The best one can do is demonstrate the performance of various models that have given satisfaction, then let him try them out for himself and make his own decision.

Many of my casting pupils eager to buy a salmon fly rod are puzzled by the number of different types, all of a length, which are nowadays on offer. Indeed, I was myself, by the variety advertised by my friends Bruce & Walker, the famous rod makers. But all that Ken Walker would say darkly when taxed on the subject was:

"You'd be surprised."

I was. Shortly after that conversation, five salmon fishers who share a beat on Tweed turned up at Bruce & Walker's premises in Huntingdon to buy a new rod apiece. They were offered the choice of seventeen rods and spent the afternoon trying them out (all for fishing the same water). At the finish each angler bought a different model! So, you can understand what I mean.

Having acquired a rod – and probably paid the earth for it – do look after it. Never Spey cast with it, even for short practice sessions, without *taping the joints*. And when you do so, do it thoroughly.

Speycasting is (or should be) a series of curves. Except for the final power stroke there are no straight lines. The curving, twisting action of the rod tends to loosen the ferrules. Exacerbated by the expansion of the air inside hollow rods of circular construction caused by the heat of a summer day, these loosened joints will result in loss of casting power and if not checked and tightened in time may cause breakage. During a day's fishing, remember to check the alignment of your rod rings from time to time, they provide the first indication that the joints are working loose underneath the tape – which will stretch on a hot day.

There are people in the tackle trade, seemingly ignorant of Speycasting, who will tell you that rod-taping is unnecessary. Ignore them. You have paid quite enough for your rod; don't risk breaking it because of foolishness.

N.B. As I was writing this chapter, Ken Walker informed me that a patent had been applied for concerning a new hexagon-shaped spigot and socket which, it is hoped, will entirely eliminate the need for rod-taping.

At the time of going to press I have spent some time trying out this new joint and can report most favourably. The test rod has stood up to a good deal of continuous Speycasting – both on the river and the casting platform – and if, as now seems likely, these ferrules continue to resist pulling apart, there can be no doubt that the time-consuming chore of taping and untaping will soon take its place in angling history.

American game angler and author, Thomas Pero (left), discusses the pros and cons of our Knott End one-piece rods with a master rod-builder, Ken Walker of Bruce & Walker Ltd, makers of the successful Hexagraph design.

With regard to the method of sticking rod joints together, Bill Arnold offers the following advice: *Hexagraph rods have a central hard core as opposed to circular rods, which are hollow. This makes a difference to the way we glue them together. First of all, by using fine sandpaper, make the male ferrule fit snugly into the female ferrule so that the two shoulders are brought together.*

*With the Hexagraph rod you will need to inscribe a groove down the male ferrule using a pointed tool. I use a bradawl. This has to be done, to make an escape route which lets the air out, otherwise the joints will spring apart because of the air put under compression. With hollow, circular rods, this doesn't occur.*

*The glue to use is a two part Epoxy, such as Araldite. Mix it*

*thoroughly. Apply to the male ferrule and join the two sections together with a twisting action, making sure the rod rings are in line. It is as simple as that – saving hours of setting together, taping up and, later, untaping and breaking down, besides cluttering up the inside of your motor.*

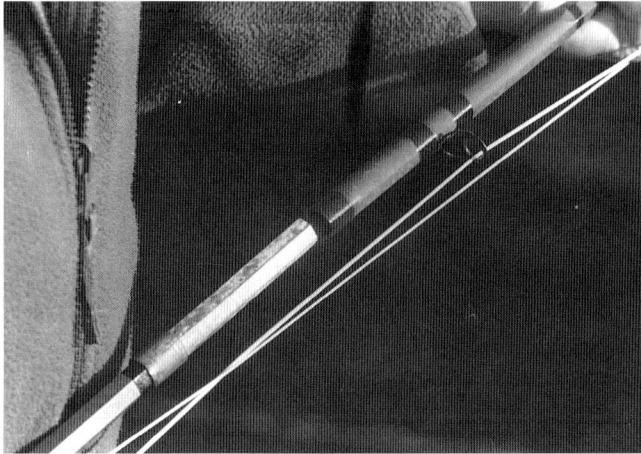

New hexagraph-shaped spigot and socket.

*Travelling with mounted rods.* The trick is to run them from bonnet to roof, making sure they are held down firmly at the front with elastic luggage-straps, either to a bull-bar or small rings which you can easily fit to the bumper with self-tapping screws. We use magnetic clamps on the bonnet, and thumb-screw clamps on the roof.

Since most salmon fly fishermen persist in using an overhead cast most rod-makers mark up the line sizes accordingly.

Generally speaking, you will find that for Speycasting you need a size larger than for casting overhead. So, if a rod is marked for a Number 10 line it will probably Spey cast better with the larger (and heavier) Number 11 line. (It is essential that the rod does sufficient work.) But this is only a rough guide. Nothing takes the place of practical experience. The only way to discover what rod suits you best and what size of line will help you make an effortless Spey cast is to *try it out on water.* You will learn nothing from waggling it about in the shop. Some makers and tackle dealers have water available for rod testing. Some don't.

Never buy a rod untested straight off the hook or through the post – unless you are assured it can be returned if your test casts reveal a weakness.

When testing rods professionally, I have spent many long hours day after day trying out against each other nearly every make of salmon rod in the world. Naturally, all sorts of claims are made by the various makers, but in my experience, *provided they are fitted with the correct weight of line*, and although, naturally, some will do slightly better than others, *top quality* rods don't vary all that much.

My final advice on buying a rod is this: first learn to Speycast well. Then go to a maker who will give you the opportunity to test several different rods so that you can find the action that seems to suit you best. When you know how to use a rod you will soon be able to decide on what is best for *you*. I have no intention of trying to blind you with science about rod construction. Such is the speed of advance in technology that anything I write now may well be obsolete by the date of publication. Enough to say that at the time of writing, having given it the most tremendous work-out that any fly rod can have had in recent years, Hexagraph construction has seemed to me to be more resilient than its tubular counterparts.

But I repeat: all the top quality rods I have tested will Speycast well enough. And I am not referring simply to how *far* they will cast.

Most writers in the angling press put too much emphasis on casting distance. "How far will it cast?" is the cry when they set out to choose a rod. Listen, few if any modern top quality rods are lacking in potential distance. Frankly, most of them are too good for most of the anglers using them. It is not so much a question of how far your *rod* can cast, but how far *you* can cast.

And having said that, let me offer you a word of advice. Don't let the quest for casting distance become obsessive. Some anglers (possessed I think by a competitive spirit) think of little else. Concentrate first and foremost on safety and accuracy. On most salmon rivers, distance is far from being all-important.

To be able to throw a long line plumes up the will, feeds the self-confidence and gives no end of quiet satisfaction, but when we are trying to catch fish a *very* long line is seldom needed.

Yes, yes, I know there are exceptions, and I know where most of these places are, certainly in Britain for I have fished them; but of all the salmon I have caught, I can remember few that were hooked on a cast of over thirty-five yards and most have been caught on a much shorter line than that. This was not due to incompetence. In the days before my hands fell to pieces because of operations on solar keratoses,* I demonstrated a lot of long

*Footnote. To those of my readers who suffer a similar affliction I recommend the protection of cotton mittens when on the water. They have the added advantage of assisting one's grip, and so, make the hand-tailing of salmon much easier. Through the kind intervention of the famous American angler, Lefty Krch, I now own a pair of "sungloves", ideal protectors available from Mangrove Co., 4027.7 street S.E., Calgary, Alberta, Canada T2G 2Y9.

distance Spey casts of thirty-five to forty yards, made with a standard fifteen-foot rod and Number 11 double-tapered line, but I have almost never needed to cast anything like that distance when fishing. It is comforting to have extra casting range in reserve for those rare occasions when we *have* to stretch our muscles, and to know that our tackle is capable of responding, but it is in reserve where, most of the time we are fishing, it should stay.

There is one thing to especially guard against in salmon-fishing: not to attempt long casts until you are perfect with the short line. It has a certain fascination for us all, so the habit is easily acquired. Even experienced anglers are often too anxious to throw a long line, and I must confess that I sometimes try to raise my salmon with the line well out, although frequently failing in the attempt. One will have better sport by remembering the following rule: Throw only the length of line you can throw well.

Edmund W. Davis,
*Salmon-Fishing on the Grand Cascapedia* (1904)

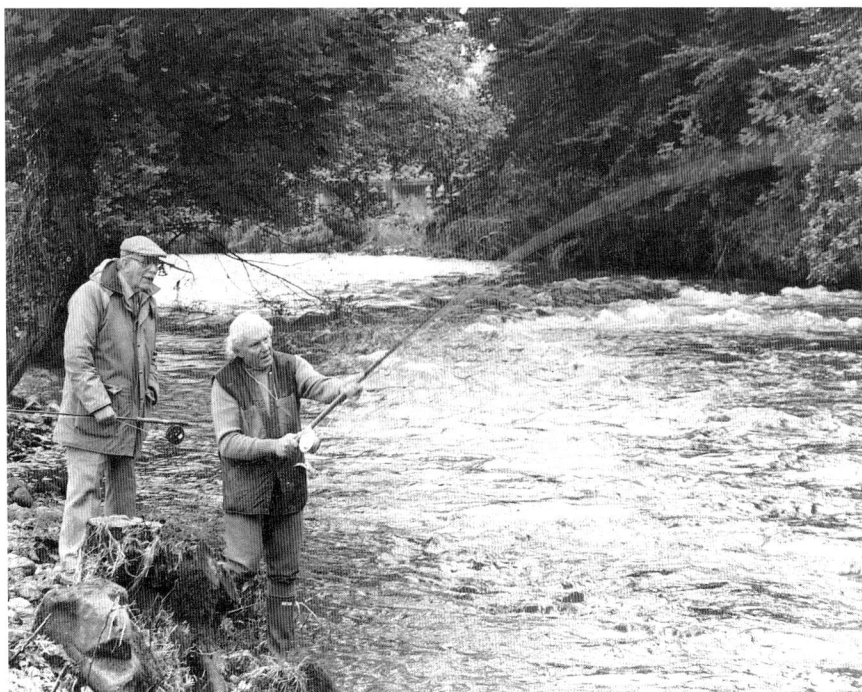

The author demonstrating some distance Speycasting with double-handed and single-handed rods at a Welsh Angling Fair.

His assistant is an old friend, Major David Monckton, formerly of the Parachute Regiment, who in 1944 was badly wounded and awarded the M.C. and D.S.O. for gallantry.

Never go salmon fishing with only one rod! In the picture a prototype rod has failed the crucial test of a long Spey cast. If you have no back-up rod handy to fill the gap, all sorts of accidents can deprive you of your sport and ruin a day's fishing. But breakage is not the only reason for taking a second rod with you. From a practical, hunting, fish-catching point of view, it frequently pays to put up two rods with different lines: floater, and floater with sink-tip; floater with sink-tip, and quick sinker – so that you can vary your attack according to strengths of current, water temperature and general weather conditions.

To be able to change quickly from one method of fly fishing to another, without having to break down your tackle in order to make the change, is a great time-saver and will undoubtedly encourage you to do what otherwise you might not have done.

In the long term this will help you to catch fish – as it does me.

*Note*: See comment on avoidance of spare spools (p. 195).

Anyway, you will only increase your casting distance as you improve your roll casting, on which all your Spey casts depend. As your wrists get stronger, particularly your bottom wrist, distance will come automatically. To help you appreciate this and to assist you on the river, measure out 20 yards of your casting line and mark it with a streak of red nail varnish. Put another marker at 25 yards and another at 30 yards. Now, when you are fishing, you will know to a foot how much line you have out.

The need to practise cannot be over-stressed. Any piece of water will do, so long as you can form the loop of a roll cast. To help keep you within your limits when fishing, determine the maximum distance you can roll cast – *over* the water, without the belly of the line touching down first – and mark this distance with a green streak. You will find to your delight that regular practice sessions will soon enable you to rub off this marker and replace it a yard or two further up the line.

The ability to cast a long and accurate line should be the aim of every salmon angler, but when you are trying to catch fish, don't sacrifice accuracy in an attempt to increase your distance. Never cast a yard further than you *have* to. Never try to cast a yard further than you *can*.

Accuracy of presentation and control of the fly are more important than striving for excessive distance.

That women by and large make highly successful salmon fishers I think most of us would agree, and the reason for their success has been hotly debated. This is no place to discuss my friend Professor Peter Behan's intriguing theory concerning the efficacy of the female pheromone, beyond saying that male readers with a sense of humour will find it highly diverting, and that anyone interested can read all about it in *Salmon and Women* (1990), but

Dr Malcolm Greenhalgh writing recently in the angling press had this to say:

> Whilst not decrying entirely the possibility of some feminine hormonal advantage, I am sure that the main reason for their success is that ladies are far more careful and precise in the way their flies behave. On average, they are more meticulous in the way they fish, whereas men on average tend to be more concerned about how far they can cast.

I think there is a lot of truth in that.

*     *     *

About the performance of fly lines, elaborate claims are made from time to time; but of the lines I have tested, none has been outstanding. Bearing in mind that I probably make more fly casts during a season's fishing and teaching than many anglers make in a lifetime, it will be understood that the lines my pupils and I use get a pretty thorough hammering. As with fly rods, in my opinion there is little to choose between any of the double taper floating lines made by the few *top-grade* manufacturers.

Floating lines are mostly of a very light colour and I seem to get on as well with one as with another. Several different makes accompany me to the river for fishing and also to the casting platforms for teaching, and all have served me well. When we come to *sinking* lines, however, there is a dramatic change in the script.

As with various other items of fishing tackle (too numerous to mention without lengthy digression), the tackle-makers' thinking behind their design of sinking lines beggars belief. Every diver I have talked to has confirmed that the least visible colour underwater is white. And what do the tackle-makers turn out? Lines of dark brown, dark green and even of black – the most visible of all colours underwater, as most salmon fly-tyers have learned to their advantage. A salmon does not lurk near the surface of a river looking down (when a dark colour would be the most suitable camouflage for the back of a fish lying below, as indeed it would be for a sunk fly line), it lies close to the bottom, looking up. Obviously, the most practical colour for an underwater line is white, for this makes it less visible against the sky.

Clearly it is for this reason that natural selection has given most fish white bellies: it helps protect them from predators swimming underneath. For the same reason, the white undersides of predatory plunge-diving seabirds makes them less visible to the sprats and other small fry on which they feed.

An interesting exception is the fish-eating Arctic skua, which Nature has coloured dark brown underneath. A bird of piratical habits, it makes its living by robbing the smaller plunge-diving birds such as terns and kittiwakes. Frightened by the swooping skua's threatening appearance, a terrified tern drops its newly-caught sprat – which the skua immediately retrieves and swallows.

Learning from Nature is something the tackle-makers seem able to resist.

*    *    *

The use of a white sinking line revolutionizes early spring and late autumn salmon fishing. In addition to helping avoid disturbance, its colour enables you *to see what you are up to*. You know instantly how well you are casting. After struggling with a dark-coloured line, which is almost invisible against a background of trees and other bankside vegetation, you will find it a revelation.

*Historical item*
Nineteen hundred years ago, Plutarch wrote:

Take care that the hairs which reach to the hook should seem as white as possible, for the whiter they are the less they are seen in the water.

*   *   *

## THE SINK-TIP LINE

If, at the end of fishing out a cast, a sink-tip line has swung into slack water and the tip has sunk, it may be necessary – especially when fishing a biggish fly – to bring sink-tip, leader and fly to the surface by rolling straight back down-stream in the manner of sunk-line fishing (see Chapter IX). But once this has been done, a correctly-designed sink-tip line should be as easy to roll over as a fully floating (or, for that matter, a fully sinking) line of the same AFTM number.

Not every angler, however, finds this possible.

Among many anglers I have spoken to, the sink-tip line seems to have caused a certain amount of confusion. This is due, I have discovered, to a widespread ignorance of sink-tip flyline design.

Perhaps this is not so surprising. Of over twenty-five tackle dealers I once telephoned at random, not one could explain to me what special quality, if any, a sink-tip line should possess to make it suitable for Speycasting.

Small wonder then, that even very experienced fly-casters come to me in acute distress, thinking that their Speycasting has somehow, suddenly, gone on the twist – an unfortunate simile, perhaps, but for them depressing enough in fact.

"There's something gone wrong with my Speycasting," a friend complained recently. "I've just bought a new double tapered fly line, but trying to turn it over in a roll cast is like trying to cast a bucket. It must be *me* at fault. Surely it can't be the line?"

But it was.

He had bought the wrong type of sink-tip line, and on the water the answer was only too painful – rollcasting it *was* like trying to cast a bucket !

In passing, I may say that nobody told me anything about any of this; I had to learn it from first principles. As I have passed it on to many of my pupils, so I am passing it on to my readers in an attempt to be helpful.

The impression I am left with is that the fact of there being two types of sink-tip line on the market is not generally understood. (There may be more; but I know of two.) *One can be turned over easily in a roll cast, and the other can't.* All too often, people who have bought the wrong type of "floater/sinker" line, lose confidence in their roll and Speycasting, not realising that the fault lies in the line, not in their technique. And in my opinion this is the reason why, from time to time, the sink-tip line gets savaged in the angling press.

The "rogue" line responsible for the Speycasters' criticisms is intended for overhead casting. It is, in effect, a form of "weight-forward" line; suitable for overhead casting with a double-haul technique, but entirely unsuitable for Speycasting. Unfortunately, many dealers and most anglers I have talked to seem not to be aware of this, and the line-makers – either from ignorance or cynicism – refrain from including any explanation on their sales material. So that the innocent (albeit ignorant) Speycaster may buy a "rogue" sink-tip line unaware that it is completely alien to his system of casting.

Burn the following advice on your brain with letters of bright gold:

> For sink-tip Speycasting it is essential to use a line the weight of whose sinking part equals that of a similar length of an all-floating or an all-sinking line of the same AFTM number.

My book *Salmon Fishing* explains in detail the principle of sink-tip fly fishing. Here I need only affirm that, together with my friends, I use correctly-designed sink-tip lines with great success.

A SINK-TIP LINE GUIDE

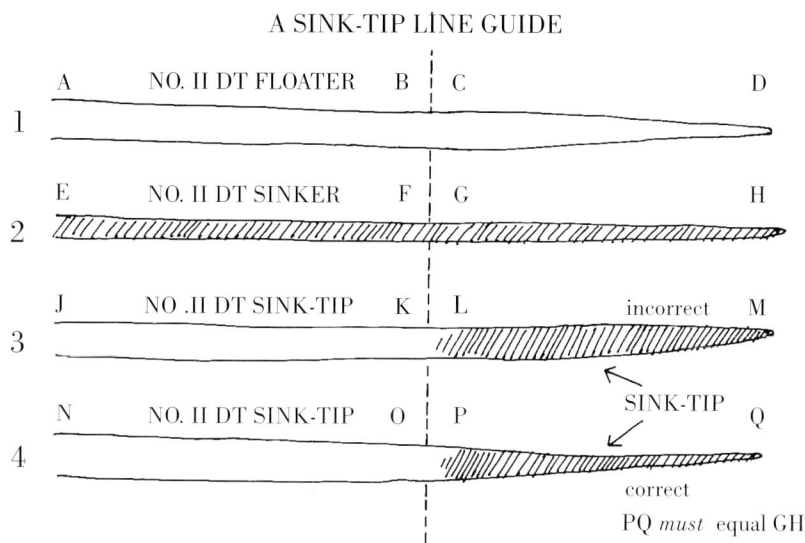

In weight: AB=EF=JK=NO

In weight: CD = GH = PQ, but *not* LM, which in thickness is the same as CD and therefore too heavy to turn over.

For the Speycaster, No. 3 is the "rogue" sink-tip line, which will produce the "bucket" effect. It is totally unsuitable for Speycasting, being intended for "weight forward" overhead casting.

Line 1 is the same weight as line 2 – although, being an all-sinker, line 2 is *thinner*.

The floating portions of lines 3 and 4 are also equal in weight, as they are to the equivalent lengths of lines 1 and 2.

But line 3 is tapered in the same way as line 1, and therefore the sinking part will be too heavy for Speycasting.

For it to turn over smoothly, line 4 must have a sinking part that equals a similar length in lines 1 and 2 (CD and GH). The abrupt taper PQ ensures this.

*Note*: Before buying a sink-tip line, examine the sinking portion (see PQ above). If suitable for Speycasting the difference in line diameter between floating and sinking parts should speak for itself.

## AS IT WAS

When I was a young man I used three silk lines for salmon fly fishing:

1   Totally ungreased and therefore full sinker.

2   Totally greased and therefore full floater.

3   Greased except for the last two to four yards, thus being a floater with sink-tip. The length fished free of grease varying according to the strength of the water, unwanted grease being rubbed off with a piece of earth.

It worked splendidly and for all intents and purposes this is how I fish today. Except that nowadays with modern materials, I use four lines instead of three: floater; sinker, and two floaters with sink-tips – one long tip, one short tip, to suit variations in water height – each on its own reel. (No spare spools for me! See p.195.)

Twisted horsehair tapered fly-line, c.1850

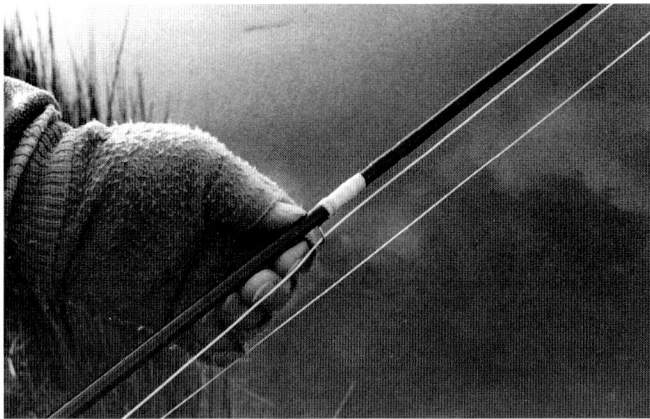

Rod joints taped (single-handed rod)

To avoid poking a companion in the face, here are two safe ways of carrying a fly rod. Pointing forward when walking in front. Pointing backwards when bringing up the rear.

BUT remember that a modern carbon rod is a great conductor of electricity. Watch out for those dreadful pylons that straddle the countryside, and for warning signs such as the one above. Overhead electric cables have killed or injured too many anglers already.

As a result of a brilliant reverse Spey cast right across the Stjordal river, to a solitary rock at extreme range (the lure I was using happened to be one of your $2\frac{1}{2}$-inch tandem sea trout jobs) I hooked a fish, which – instead of the 48-pounder I expected – turned out to be a brown trout of 7 oz. It thrashed on the surface, which was faintly embarrassing, since my rod (your rod) could have pulled an armoured car from the deep with no trouble.

Retiring to the shore, I took up my small trout rod, intent on catching a few brownies for a picnic tea. The river was fast, high and burly, but there was a quieter place three yards out, and another rock. I cast a size 14 double Peter Ross above this rock, into two feet of water . . . I expect you've guessed what happened. A 6 lb grilse took the fly. It got out into the torrent, and I had a hell of a job to extricate it. The Speycaster would have lifted it out like a plummet . . .

David Burnett (from a letter)

## II  THE ROLL CAST

OF ALL our casts, the roll cast is the most valuable and is the first cast I teach any aspiring fly fisher, no matter what methods he wishes to learn. There are, of course, *two* roll casts one changing direction to the left, one changing direction to the right.

The reason for the two different roll casts is surely obvious: it prevents getting hung-up. If we draw our line back on our right-hand side, we can only cast cleanly to the *left* of our starting point. If we tried to cast to the right, the loop would cross over and, as it straightened out, would catch up with leader and fly every time.

Similarly, we shall get hung-up every time if we try to roll cast to the left when our line is lying on our left-hand side.

Usually, to make these two different roll casts, experienced anglers change hands – having either the right hand up the rod or the left hand up the rod as the case may be: casting to the right from the left shoulder, or to the left from the right shoulder. But I am suggesting that these rather old-fashioned methods have several disadvantages. (*Not* that we shouldn't be able to roll cast from either shoulder, we *should*, but that is something in addition to what I recommend.) If we aspire to making ourselves into thoroughly competent and versatile fly casters, we must be able to roll cast either right or left *from the same shoulder.*

Then, once we have mastered both roll casts from the right shoulder we should master them from the left shoulder, and that goes on to include *all* the casts described in this book. We shall then be fully ambidexterous – (and eligible for my Order of Merit!).

These two roll casts are the basis of all our Speycasting. But there are times when a Spey or a double Spey is unnecessary and we can fish down a stretch of water perfectly well using only a roll cast. It is, for instance, a most practical cast when we are wading down a narrow, tree-girt run for sea trout at night. The fly never comes behind us and gets hung up; indeed, never leaves the water until the forward stroke is made. It is so safe and, if properly executed, so stealthy. When driven forward, as it should be, *above* the water, it lands with no greater splash than a perfect overhead cast and causes the very minimum of disturbance.

Generally speaking, we can roll cast an angle of about 30° to the right or left. When the angle becomes greater than that, or we are unable to form a loop owing to wind or bank obstructions, Speycasting becomes obligatory. But what we must remember is that the final power stroke of all our Spey casts (whether single or reverse-single, double or reverse-double) is nothing other than a roll or reverse roll cast.

All that Speycasting really amounts to is putting our line in such a position that we can form a loop and roll cast it in whatever direction we wish. Speycasting, in other words is re-directed roll casting. And thought of in that light, stripped of all its former mystique, Speycasting becomes instantly understandable and, when we have nailed down the two roll casts, so easy both to perform and to teach.

For reasons that will (I hope) become clear as we burrow our way through this book, the advantages of being able to make these casts off the same shoulder – instead of having to change shoulders according to whichever bank we are on – are huge, and however difficult and disheartening my reader may find his early attempts at reverse roll-casting, I urge him to persevere. As I have implied in a previous chapter, he will find himself amply rewarded.

Before we start on roll casting instruction, however, there are one or two questions that need to be answered. For instance, what is it that makes a roll cast possible? Why can we roll cast on unfrozen water but not on ice? Why, sometimes, when we make the forward stroke of a roll or Spey cast, does our line crack like a whip resulting, unless we are lucky, in the loss of our fly?

Well, there is one answer to all of this: the surface tension of the water.

The moment a line touches the surface of the water, *if only for a fraction of a second*, the surface tension grips it all the way along like a row of little hands. On ice, or on the lawn, surface tension is absent. There are no "little hands" to grip and control the speed of our loop as it unfolds, with the result that the line scriggles up and finishes in a curlywig.

It is these "little hands" that control our line as we propel it in all our Roll, Spey and Double-Spey casting. If, as we form our loop, we do not allow sufficient line to kiss the water at the vital moment of our power stroke, the line will crack and as like as not, we shall lose our fly.

From my experience, this does not seem to be generally understood. At various shows, I have watched Speycasting demonstrations by "experts" that at times sounded like pheasant shoots!

When you are wading you are unlikely to be bothered much by line-cracking; the nearer you are to the surface, the more readily the line lies on the water and is gripped by the "hands". Difficulty comes when you are Speycasting from a high bank, especially in a strong wind, which may lift a vital yard or so of line off the water. Not that a great length of line is necessary, just a yard or so near the rod point makes all the difference. It is a question of watching the loop out of the corner of your eye and timing the forward stroke accordingly – that is, not being too hasty. Most defective casting results from trying to be too quick and rushing the finish of the cast before the loop has swung back far enough for the "little hands" to get a grip.

All this may be the reason why so many anglers cast "out of their bellies" with their hands held far too low. By *chance* (because I don't think many of them know why they are doing it) the curl of their loop is nearer the water, which helps to banish line-cracking. This may avoid one fault, but creates others, and anglers who continue with this technique will never raise their casting standards above the mediocre.

In *Salmon Fishing* by Eric Taverner *et al* (1931) – which, when I was young, was the salmon-fisher's bible – there is the following statement:

> Both kinds of Spey cast are apt to throw the line on the water before the fly and also to disturb the pool unduly . . .

and it goes on to say:

> It is a very common fault in those accustomed to overhead casting to raise their arms as high as they naturally would in that cast; but in

Speycasting, double or single, the upper hand should not be lifted higher than the ear.

Now, why on earth should those anglers of yesterday have chosen to restrict themselves in this way? It is quite illogical. Assuming that all the rods used are the best of their kind, a longer line can be roll cast, and with greater ease, with a 15 ft. rod than with a 10 ft. rod; and with a 20 ft. rod than with a 15 ft. rod, because of the size of the loops thrown. But, by raising our arms to the height I recommend in the "key" position, we can get results with a 15 ft. rod that equal those of a 17 ft. rod if the latter is used with the traditional technique.

It was probably due to an imperfect understanding of the principles of roll casting (including the important part played by the "little hands") combined with the weight of their heavy greenheart and split cane rods, that the old-timers raised the right hand no higher than the ear.

Just bear in mind that only a few years ago a noted angler and casting champion wrote:

The double-handed cast . . . is really no more than the single-handed cast with the lower hand taking the weight of a rod that is too heavy to be used with one hand.

Very well, all this was understandable. But not in the light of modern knowledge and equipment. We should be wiser today, our rod materials being so much lighter and more efficient than the weaver's beam of old. If, as I have proved many times, we can throw a longer and less fish-disturbing line, with less effort than hitherto, then that is what instructors should be teaching. But many of them are not, and that is one of my bones of contention. As I can see for myself every season on the rivers, just like those salmon fishers of a bygone age most people are still casting "out of their bellies". And as if hammering the point home, that is how they cast when, frustrated by their inability to achieve any sort of distance, they come to me for instruction.

This picture sequence and the one following which show four stages in a roll cast and a single Spey cast, illustrate exactly what I mean by "casting from the belly".

This is a really dreadful roll cast. The misshapen loop has resulted in the line flopping down on the water not a yard from the rod top.

It was pictures like these that first set me on the golden journey – if not to Samarkand, at least towards finding something more appropriate to present-day tackle. It seemed absurd that anglers with all the advantages of modern materials should still be shackled to such old-fashioned techniques.

When I first tried to scatter some fresh seed it fell on stony ground. What did *I* know about it? The experts knew best.

But I stuck at it. Having nothing better to do, I spent hours on the water every day, practising. Gradually the technique evolved that I teach today – and have tried

to explain in these pages.

Here the right hand never rises above shoulder height. The left hand is being pulled backwards in what masquerades as a power stroke, and the final loop will have a result as calamitous as that shown in the previous sequence.

We start a roll cast with line straight out across the water. The rod is horizontal – the position from which all our casts should start, and in which they should all finish.

*Note*: On the river our line will probably be stretching downstream at the dangle; and, if we are wading, the rod tip will be almost touching the surface.

The rod is raised – *not* vertically, but to the right in the shape of a crescent moon.

Tilted to the right to keep the line a couple of yards or so clear of the body, the rod is brought *slowly* up and back. The line follows, gliding across the surface. Don't hurry this stroke. This is nothing like the start of an overhead cast. *The line must not leave the water.* Take your time. There is no rush. Remember my axiom: In the entire range of roll and Spey casting there is never any hurry. (Even when fishing high density lines, although made with split-second timing, our casts are graceful, fluid and unhurried.)

Here the rod is approaching the "key" position – tilted at 2 o'clock to the right and coming up to an angle of 2 o'clock behind – but the reel is still too low and has to be raised a few more inches yet.

*Note*: The left hand is kept in close to the right shoulder – *not* pushed out in front, a very common mistake.

*Note also*: In this posed picture the author has omitted to hold the line firmly against the rod butt under the right forefinger. This is a fault very much to be avoided. On the river we shall almost always be holding a yard or two of slack line under our finger ready to be shot when the cast is made.

At this point the rod has gone through the "key" position and, gathering speed, is coming forward forming a loop of line preparatory to the power stroke.

The rod has been checked with a strong flick from both wrists and the line is just starting to lift off the water.

The power stroke has been made and as the rod comes down, having done its job, the loop goes shooting out.

As the loop unfolds, picking up leader and fly and taking them with it across the water towards the touchdown spot, the line begins to straighten out, while the rod returns to its horizontal starting position.

*Note*: The body has remained upright. There has been no rod pushing, or rolling of the right shoulder. It is all quite effortless.

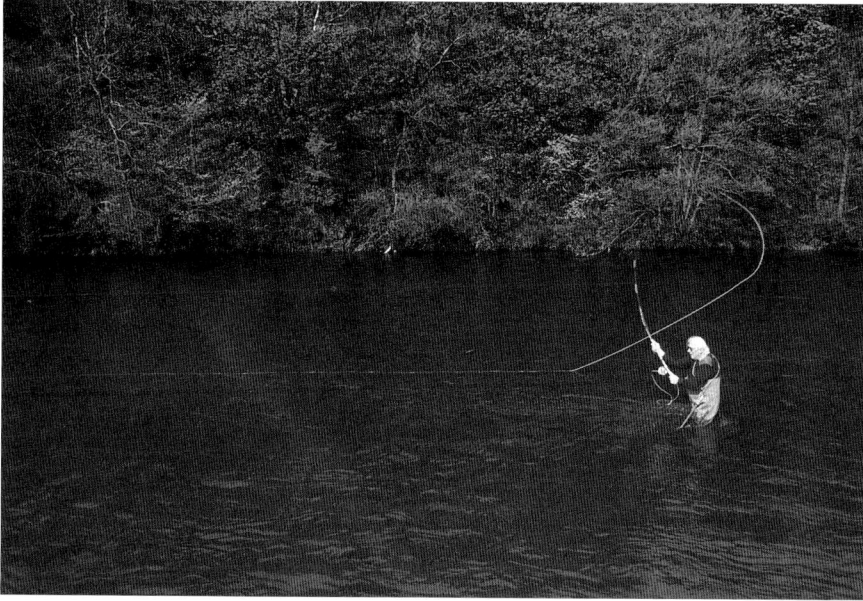

A rather sloppy roll cast on the river, purposely made to illustrate certain common faults. The rod is tilted correctly to the right, a loop has been formed and there is sufficient line close to the rod for the water tension to grip. BUT the hands are being held much too low. Clearly, the rod has not started forward from the recommended "key" position.

Here the left elbow is retreating as the left wrist is being drawn back. There is too much right hand in the cast (anglers casting like this would make strong leg-side batsmen !). The result is that the line is being propelled too low down. The belly of the line, which is already showing signs of dipping towards the surface, is likely to strike the water before the leader and fly. It is not altogether a bad cast, but then neither is it very good. Remember, this is one of the two roll casts on which all our Speycasting depends. We must do better. And we will – by going through it all and analysing it stage by stage ...

*Roll Cast, Starting Position*
Body upright. Feet at 45°. Right
foot slightly forward and pointing
in direction of the cast. Hands with
thumbs on top of the rod; ball of
left thumb in position shown above
(see also p.84).
With reference to the positioning
of the right hand on rod butts of
differing lengths, see *Rod handles*
(the right-angle triangle)
Chapter X.

Do not bend the body forward, but stand erect, and make the cast simply with the arms. It is not a graceful sight to see a person bending over and poking out his rod, with the idea that it is helping him to make a longer cast. I cannot understand why it is done, unless one thinks more power is given; on the contrary, the speed of the fly is lessened.

Edmund W. Davis, *Salmon-Fishing on the Grand Cascapedia*, (qv)

*"Key" Position, rear view*
The rod has been lifted to the right and swept round in a crescent moon curve. Reel raised to just above eye level. With both wrists "broken", the rod is tilted backwards to the 2 o'clock position, and tilted at 2 o'clock to the right. *The rod does not come to the vertical.* To ensure safety, the sideways tilt to the right is maintained throughout the cast, thus keeping the line well clear.

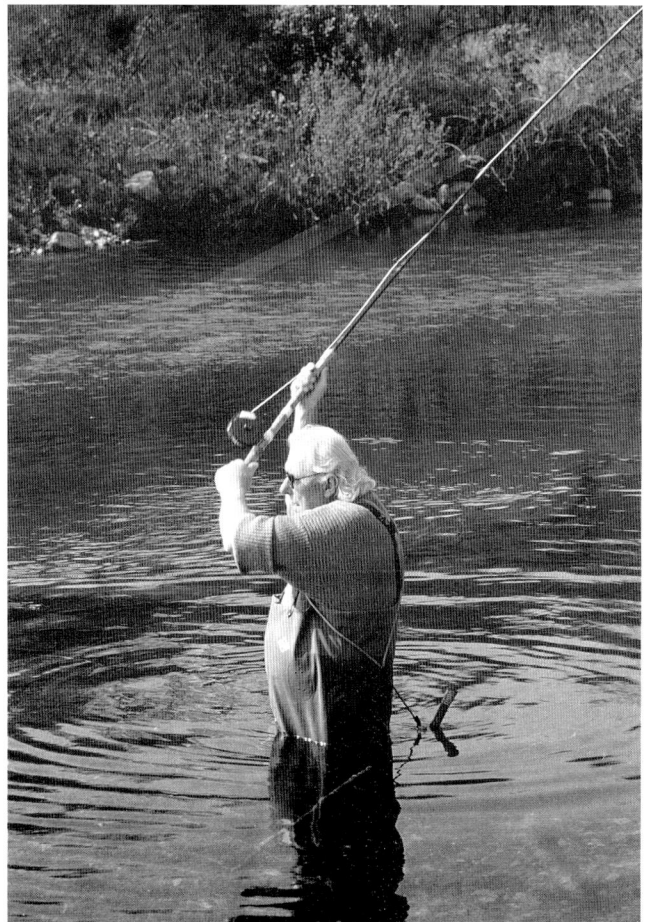

*"Key" Position, side view*
Rod tilted to 2 o'clock sideways and back. Left hand tucked back close to right shoulder, *not* pushed out in front, a common error. Note the upright stance, which is maintained throughout the cast.

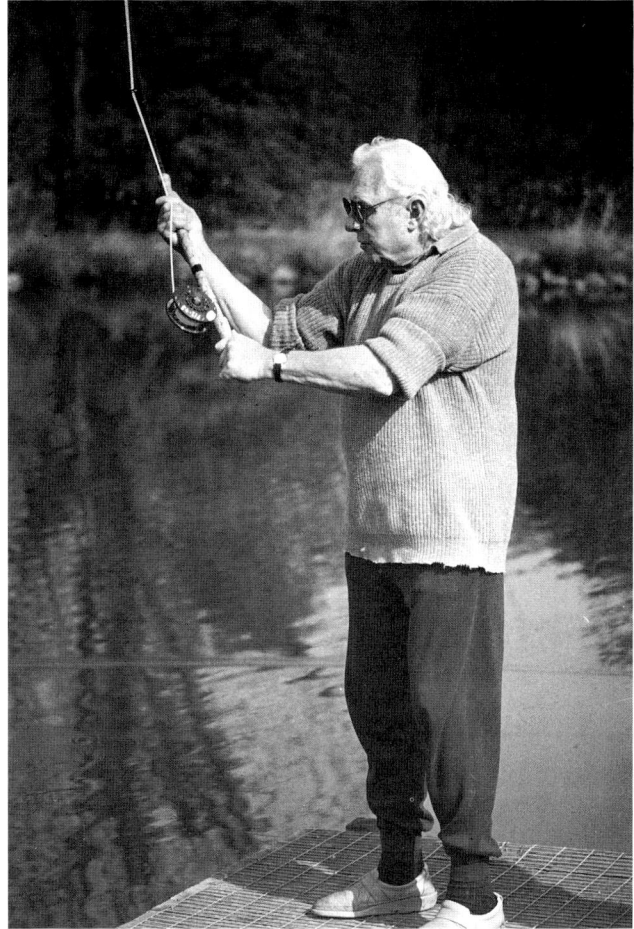

The rod has come up through the "key" position and is starting to move forward towards the power stroke. Remember, it is the *rod* that should do the work. Body, head and shoulder movements reduce the spring of the rod which propels the loop of line. A competent caster should be able to roll out a line with a glass of Scotch balanced on his head (see sequence p.90).

*The Power Stroke*

Both forearms have moved forward together and, in the next instant, both wrists will snap out of their cocked position (like the hammers on an old shotgun) to give added strength to the sudden flick as the rod passes through the angle of 11 o'clock.

*Note*: Reel tilted to the left in sympathy with rod tilted to the right.

*A Thought*: Take your wristwatch off before you start fishing, it is like wearing a small searchlight. Successful angling depends largely on attention to detail. I have often noticed the flash of light from a watch glass on a sunny day. There are times when (together with the violent glint from a varnished rod) this must disturb fish.

Perfect position at completion of power stroke. The rod (which of course does not stop or falter at any point during the cast) is coming down towards the horizontal, where it will finish up.

*Note*: Stance still upright; there has been no body or shoulder movement. Reel tilted partly sideways showing that the tilt of the rod to the right was maintained.

*Note also*: The weight has been taken on the right leg, thus avoiding any strain on the back.

59

Here, several yards of slack have been shot as the line straightens at the completion of a roll cast. Note how the belly of the line is kept high above the water. There is no chance of its landing before the fly. This cast should result in a perfect touchdown.

Such delicacy of finishing is brought about largely by the positive power of the left wrist which, by moving forward, helps to keep the line airborne.

A useful ploy that will help the beginner to cast his line above the water is to aim the power stroke above the fly's intended point of touchdown: say, halfway up a tree on the opposite bank.

In the meantime, for purposes of practising, he would be wise to make himself a "Clapperstick" …

The "Clapperstick" – a slightly more humane version of an earlier model: the "Emasculator".

The Clapperstick soon cures a pupil of old-fashioned tricks such as pulling the left hand backwards on the power stroke. The first two pictures show my friend, Mike

Mutch, using both wrists correctly. In the third picture, negative use of the left wrist induces a painful jab in the solar plexus – or thereabouts.

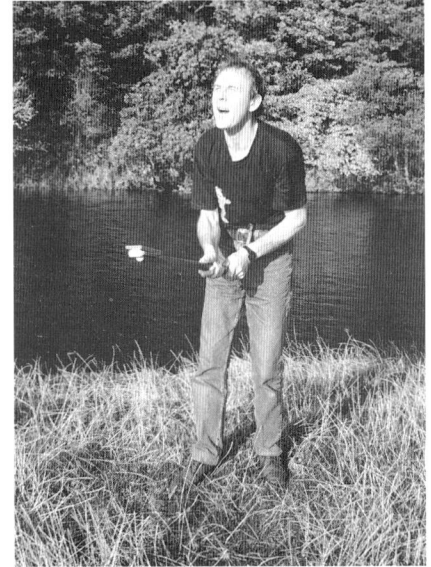

This handy little instrument can also serve as a fish measure.

Rollcasting downstream as from the left bank. Here the rod is swinging round on its way up to the "key" position – the line being kept well away from the angler's right-hand side.

Now, with the rod tilted to the right, the loop is punched out downstream well clear of the water.

*Note*: As we shall see later, this is how line and fly are brought to the surface at the start of the sunk line Speycast.

Rollcasting downstream on the right bank. This can be done only if the bank is clear. When there are bushes or other obstructions on the bank, a *reverse* roll cast is obligatory.

With sufficient line on the water for the "little hands" to grab, the roll cast can be punched out at full strength, with no danger of a whip-like crack and the concomitant loss of the fly.

Casting has an unusual effect on the mentality of the majority of anglers. David Jacques put it better than I have read it elsewhere:

> Strangely enough casting and its techniques do not make a popular subject, probably because most fly men do it so badly. Furthermore, most anglers are damn touchy on the subject, and resent any comments on their casting. You can criticize a man's choice of fly and he won't murmur. But touch him on his approach, or presentation, and he sees red.

> Quoted by Eric Horsfall Turner in *Angler's Cavalcade* (1966)

*Roll Cast Simulator*
This simple gadget guides desperate cases to the "key" position. In the picture the rod is coming up in a half-moon curve towards two o'clock. Feet at 45°. Right foot slightly forward and pointing in the direction the line is to go. As the cast is completed, weight will be taken on the right leg – which acts as a strut and protects the back.

Most people find their way into the standard roll cast without recourse to the Simulator. Once the technique of using both wrists in the forward stroke is fully understood, and attempts are made to put it into practice, the cast is easily mastered. The reverse cast (for which due to indolence Bill Arnold and I have not yet devised a suitable simulator), is another matter ...

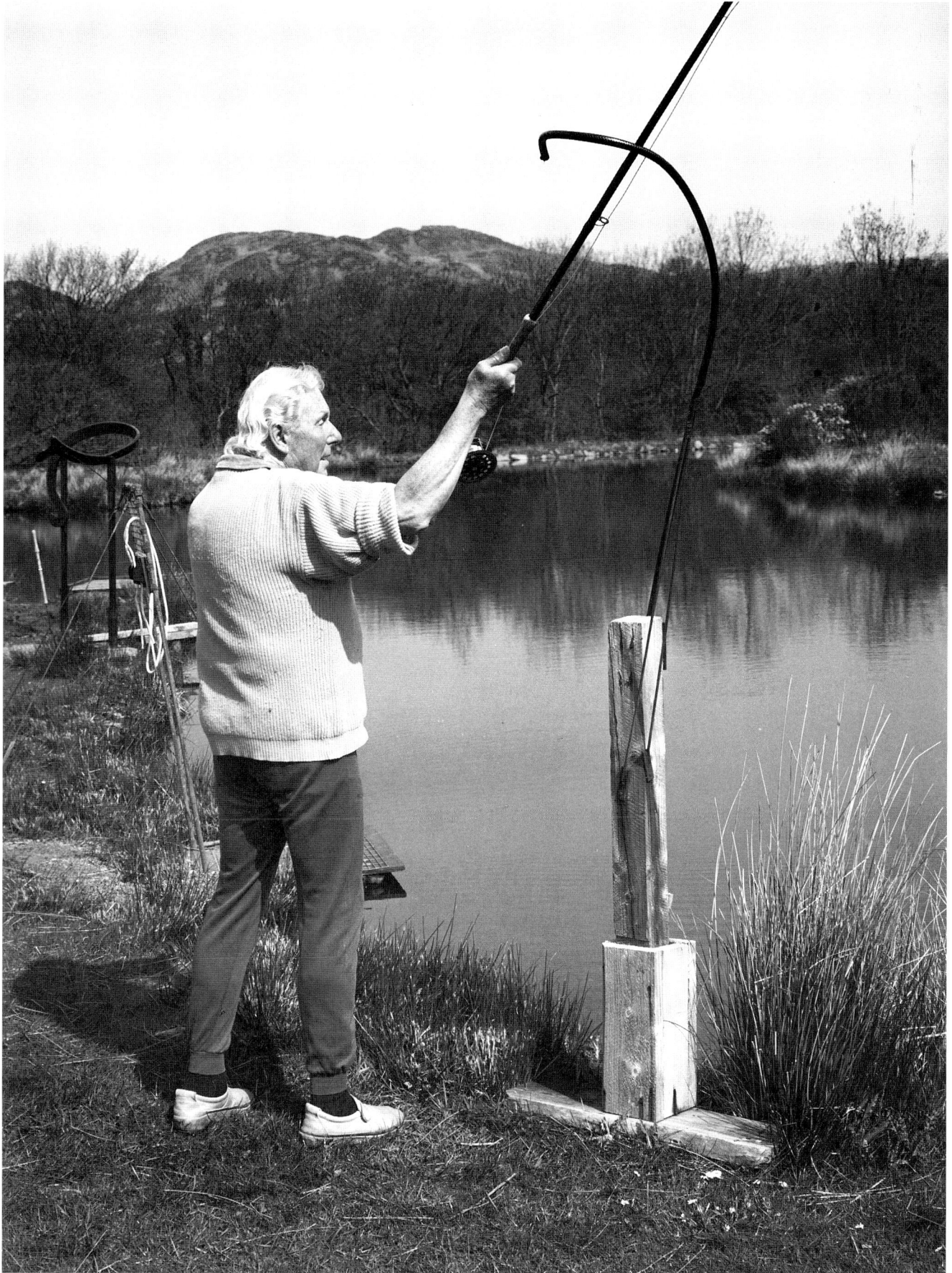

# III  THE REVERSE ROLL CAST

FOR THE beginner it is just a matter of determination. As I know, having watched so many people attempt it for the first time, reverse casting seems awkward if not downright ungainly. But take my word for it, once you get the knack it is a very simple and powerful cast. I assure you, when you have got the reverse roll cast securely kennelled you will approach the river with a new-found confidence.

There are three main points to remember:

1 The right hand straight above the top of your head in the "key" position.
2 Positive use of the left wrist.
3 Sufficient tilt of the rod (to the left).

The part played by the left wrist is all-important, but very difficult to describe. It is an upward twist to the right, as if you were using a screwdriver, at the moment the power stroke is made, so that the hand finishes up with finger-nails pointing at the sky.

It is this conscious, violent twist of the rod butt to the right, by the left hand, that gives so much extra power to the cast, as well as helping to keep the line in the air and prevent it from crashing down on the water.

In the same way that we can change direction to the left (but not to the right) when making a straightforward roll cast, we can change direction to the right (but not to the left) when making a reverse roll.

Skilful roll and reverse roll casting endows us with great benefits. It enables us to fish down many streams without recourse to Speycasting. And as we shall see later (in Chapter XI), our mastery of the valuable Contrived Loop Cast hangs on the ability to make both roll casts off the same shoulder one after the other.

Reverse roll casting across a stream. The faint line of foam where the "little hands" have held the loop is just visible.

It is worth pointing out the wealth of difference between casting when we are wading, well clear of the bank, and casting from the bank itself. Wading usually means that we can make a roll cast back downstream from whichever side we wish. A luxury denied us for most of the time we are bank fishing. As a general rule, it is roll casting from the left bank, reverse roll casting from the right.

*The Reverse Roll Cast*
We start as usual with the rod
horizontal and pointing at the fly.

But on a river the line isn't always
lying nice and straight in a steady
current. This is a posed example
on slack water of what a line often
looks like at the finish of its swing
round, however strong the river
may be. Many pools have areas of
slack water on the edge of the
current with vicious back-eddies
into which the fly will end up and
which will concertina the line. All
this wiggle needs to be evened out
before the main cast is started.
Hence the necessity for a powerful
reverse roll cast straight back
downstream.

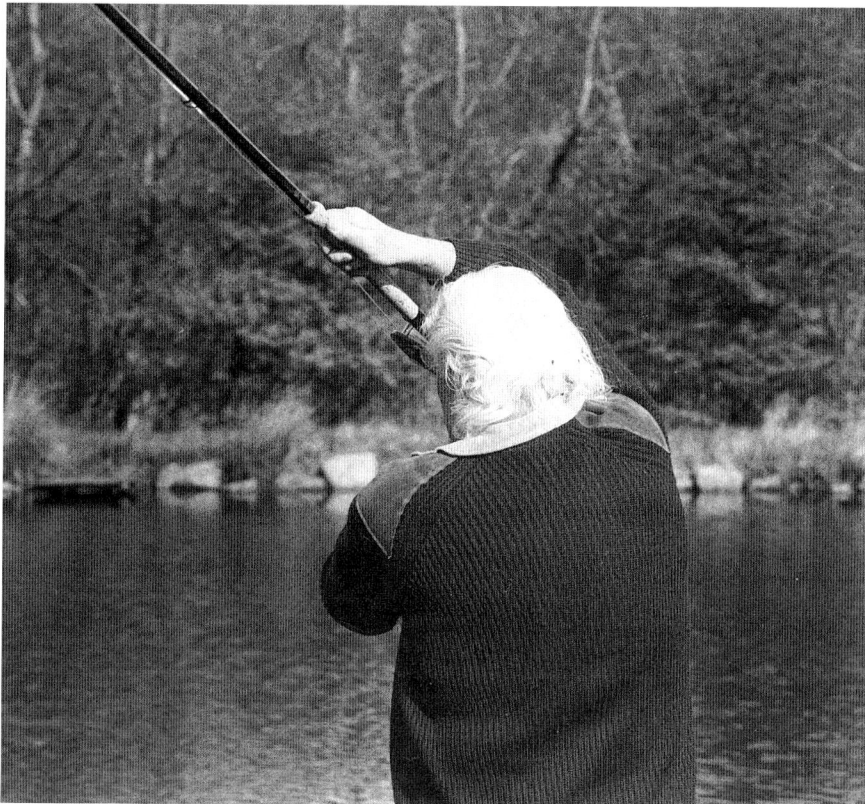

Sweep the rod round to the left, with the right arm well above the head, bringing the line gliding along the surface. Keep the rod tilted well to the left (by pushing across to the right with the left hand) and make sure it stays there during the forward stroke – or else you may get a sudden sharp shock (see p.71) !

Coming up to the reverse "key" position. But in this shot the right hand is still too far over to the left. It must move up and further round to the right, so that at the start of the forward stroke it is straight up above the centre of the head (see next picture). What we do *not* do is pretend that our right is our left arm !

Perfect reverse "key" position. Rod tilted to 2 o'clock backwards and 2 o'clock to the left – at which angle it stays until the cast is completed. *Note*: The left hand is not poking straight out in front, but is tucked in close to the right shoulder.

As the rod goes forward into the power stroke and the two wrists flick in unison; the left hand twists sharply to the right – so that it finishes up on its back, with fingernails pointing skywards. *Note*: This twist of the left wrist, which accompanies the flick, is *the key to successful reverse roll (and Spey) casting*. It gives added strength to the flick as well as "carving" the line upwards in the air and preventing the belly from hitting the surface too soon.

Finish of a reverse roll cast. Both
arms extended fully forward – the
left hand has *not* been pulled
backwards. Thumbs in position on
top of the rod. Reel half-tilted to
the right.

To make all the casts you need
from the same shoulder – will
remove you from the ranks of
everyday fly-fishers and put you
among the elite. Why ? Because
you can put out a line in conditions
that defeat most anglers and send
them scampering home.

The author demonstrates the
"screwdriver" action of the left
wrist to Ed Jaworowski, super
American fly-caster.

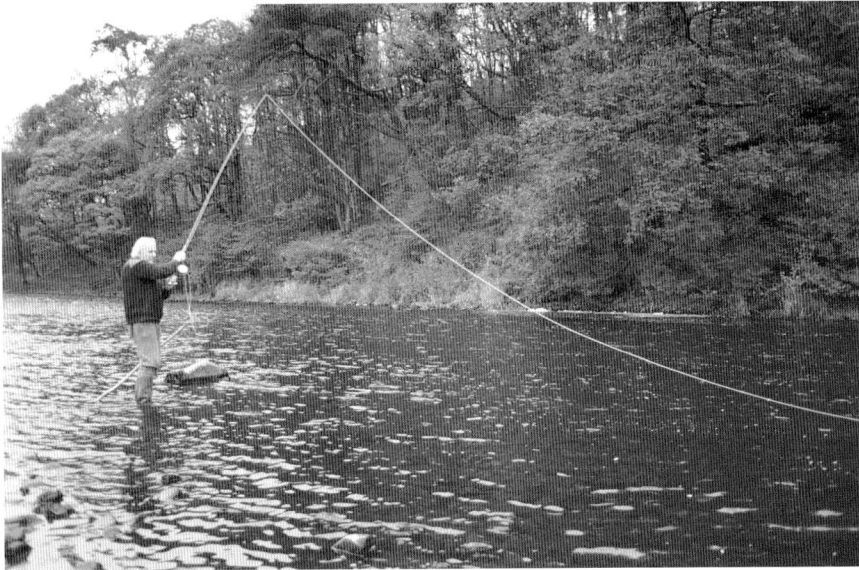

Reverse roll casting downstream to straighten out the line, or bring a sunk fly to the surface – after which it is an easy matter to go into a double Spey cast from the same shoulder. (As we shall see in Chapter VI.)

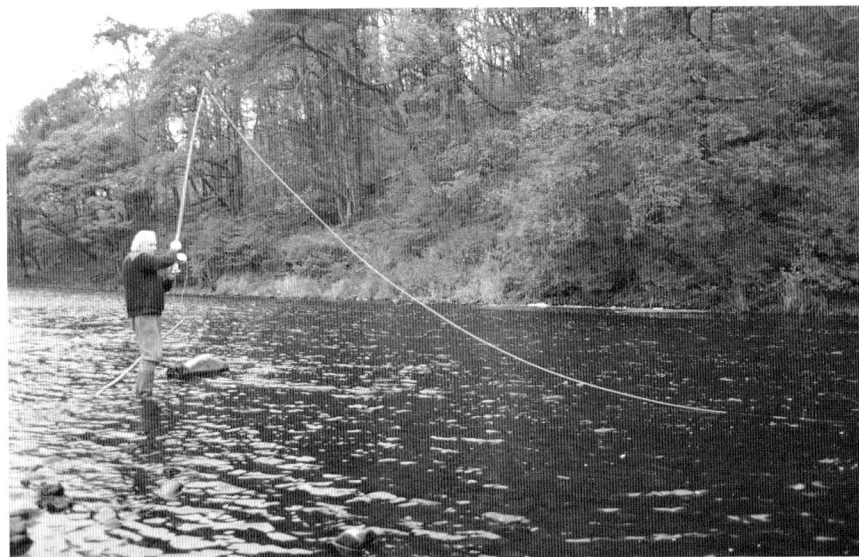

The rod is brought up on the tilt…

And kept on the tilt (an angle of about 2 o'clock to the left).

*Reverse Casting: a Warning*
When reverse casting, especially
while you are practising, *always*
wear preventers on your spectacles
and watch out for your hat. If you
bring the rod up too straight and
fail to keep sufficient tilt to the left
as you make the forward stroke, the
line may pass too close to the left
side of your head and sweep off hat
and spectacles into the water. Over
the years, Bill Arnold and I have
spent many hours in breast waders,
or the boat, poking about with
landing nets, recovering pupils' lost
property.

As I write, there is still an
expensive deerstalker lying
somewhere in the depths of Knott
End Tarn.

*A badly executed reverse roll cast*
The angler is well positioned and
standing erect, but the rod is being
brought up *much too straight*. In a
second or two, as the rod arrives at
2 o'clock immediately prior to the
forward stroke, the line will have
formed into a loop behind the
angler and to his left. There will be
nothing faulty in the "key"
position of his right hand (directly
above the centre of his head) *but*
unless he pushes the rod butt
further to the right with his left
hand *to give the rod more tilt*, the
loop will form much too close to
his body. As a result, the line in the
power stroke is likely to brush his
left ear.

It is "narrow-gutted" reverse
casts such as this that are
responsible for whisking off hats
and specs.

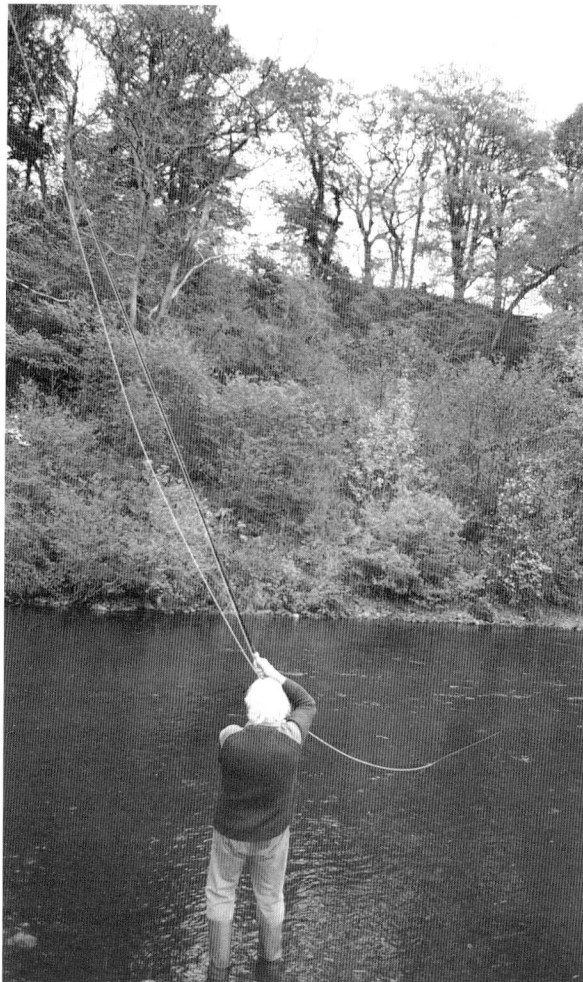

The pictures show a general fault in reverse casting – whether reverse rollcasting, reverse single Speycasting, or reverse double Spey – the angle of the rod. This has already been pointed out, but here it is shown in a rollcasting sequence.

Here the rod is too upright and the line is being drawn back almost straight towards the angler.

Now, just prior to the power stroke, the rod is nearly vertical and the line is quite likely to brush the angler's face.

He has just got away with it, but even a slight breath of downstream wind could have caused a hang-up, or something worse.

All sorts of errors can creep into summer Speycasting unpunished when floating lines and very small flies are in use. Salmon fishing becomes a different sport in early spring and late autumn when heavy tubes are to be cast safely on quick-sinking lines.

Learn the correct technique and practise it with a floating line:
Keep the line away from you.
Give yourself room.
Tilt the rod.

Wading deep and using the space available on his inshore side, this angler can substitute a reverse roll for a single Spey cast.

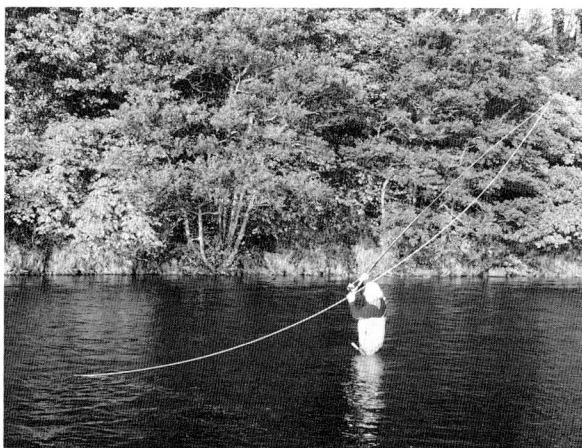

By tilting the rod and keeping the line at a safe distance he can drive his fly across the river at a thirty degree change of angle, avoiding any disturbance on his offside.

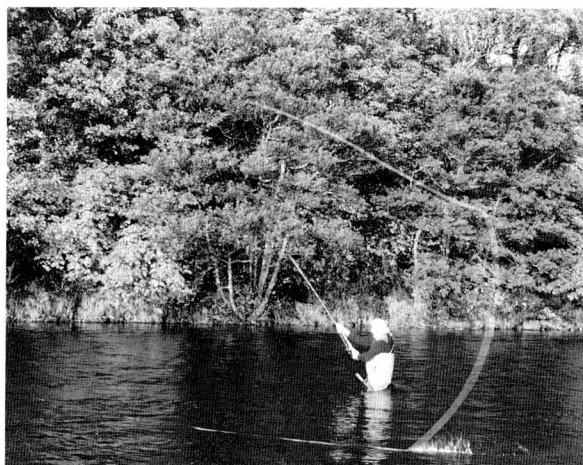

You should be able to cast equally well from either shoulder, without changing the position of the hands upon the rod. The right usually grasps the rod above the reel, with the left below. This is the position of nearly all anglers when casting from the right shoulder, whether the line is thrown in a direction diagonally to the right, straight away, or diagonally to the left; but when a cast is made from the left shoulder diagonally to the right, most salmon-anglers reverse the places of their hands. This is not at all necessary. And as it is more artistic to bend the rod towards the left shoulder and to make the cast with one's hands unchanged, why not cultivate the skill that charms – and what has more charm than the casting of a fly?

Edmund W. Davis, *Salmon-fishing on the Grand Cascapedia* (qv)

## ADVICE FROM THE PAST

> In the Spey cast, the fly is not brought behind the fisher. In order to get the line out, the rod is lifted comparatively slowly to a horizontal position. It is then moved gently from side to side, until a loop or bag of line exists between the point of the rod and the fly. This bag of line is now thrown forward, with sufficient force to carry the whole line and fly with it . . .
>
> Once you have mastered the idea and the correct timing there is no reason why you should not be able to do it.
>
> G. P. R. Balfour-Kinnear, *Flying Salmon* (1937)

I hope this will be helpful to you.

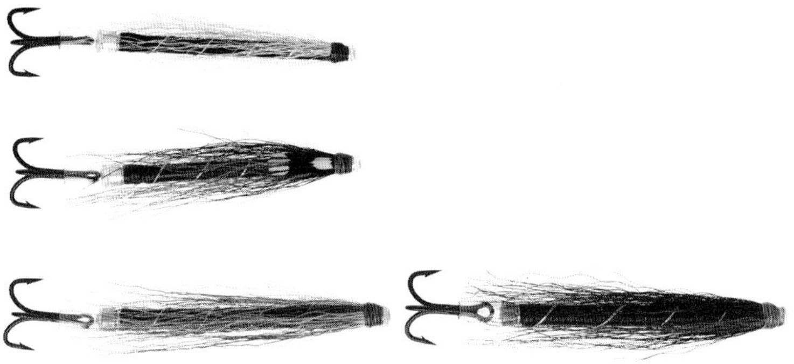

# IV  CASTING AIDS

W HEN you buy an expensive salmon fly rod, what you are paying all that money for is, primarily, a powerful and reliable spring. To get the most out of it you must treat it sensibly and give it a chance to do its job.

The pictures in this book so far have shown (and they will go on showing) that during a cast, particularly at the climax of the power stroke, the angler's body makes no bending movement. There will often be a swing from the hips, either to right or left, in sympathy with the swing of the rod, but the trunk and head will remain vertical. There will be no bobbing about, no craning forward from the waist, no rolling of the shoulder – all very common faults, which result in rod *pushing* and so dissipate energy by detracting from the spring of the rod. It is this, combined with ineffective use of the left wrist, that restricts casting distance and impairs casting accuracy.

By "accuracy" I don't mean direction alone – as we shall see, this is usually taken care of by correct placing of the right foot – it is the ability to cast a line so that in other than very windy conditions it straightens out in the air and, instead of crashing on the water, falls as lightly as the finish of a perfectly executed overhead cast. Towards this objective the avoidance of "body bobbing" plays a very important part.

There was a time when I fondly imagined I was the originator of this philosophy. Of course, as with many of my "discoveries", I was wrong. James Ogden scooped me by more than a hundred years. In *Ogden on Fly Tying* (1879), he wrote:

> The work should be done from the wrist and elbow. Never throw your body forward when making a cast, as it will not assist you to get an inch more line out.

He was right. But judging by what one has seen on river banks in the past, and is continuing unabated, this great truth was not, and is not, generally recognized.

When I was young I had the idea that if something looked good it *was* good. As one can imagine, life threw up some exceptions to this. Deadly Nightshade, for example; most women, and certain species of tropical snakes. But generally speaking it has worked out pretty well – certainly with regard to fly casting. If you watch an angler going into contortions every time he makes a throw, even though you can't see his line, you can bet a monkey he isn't getting a high rating. Whereas that girl out there in the stream, relaxed, standing straight as a spear, using only her arms without as much as a nod of her head, will be casting like a dream, with probably a couple of fish on the bank and an audience on the bridge!

As I know from years of teaching, there is nothing esoteric in any of this. Good casting lies within the compass of anyone with average muscular co-ordination prepared to learn the basic techniques, and then *practise*.

To help people to achieve this effortless mastery of the river I have, in addition to the Emasculator and the Clapperstick already mentioned, devised two other aids: the Casting Corset and the Crucifix. Both, needless to say, constructed by the great Knott End craftsman and assistant torturer, Bill Arnold.

First of all, the Corset . . .

My friend Thomas Pero, leading American magazine editor, fine all-round angler and by no means a bad Speycaster (but with a lurking shoulder-roll that needs seeing off). On a recent visit to Knott End he was introduced to the Corset ...

Fastened around shoulders, hips and to the left ankle, the corset has proved quite effective at curing body bobbing …

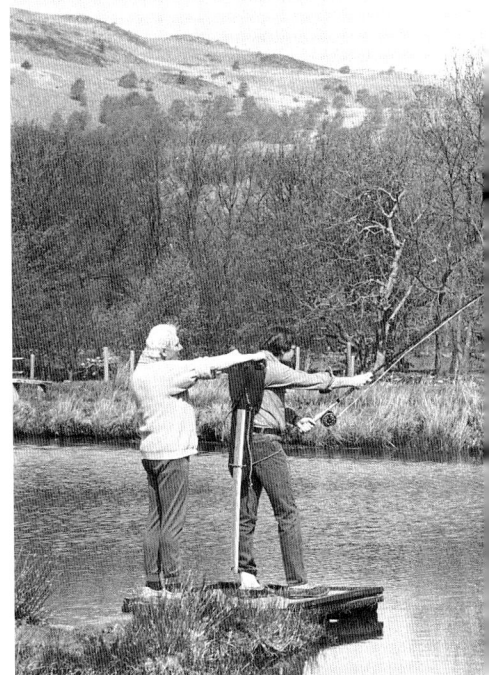

But after repeated attempts to stay upright, Thomas Pero is still trying to bob forward as he makes his power stroke. Time for sterner measures: the "Casting Crucifix" – another corrective curiously reminiscent of Tudor torture chambers …

Cords fastened with dinghy cleats hold the body upright and ensure shoulder immobility.

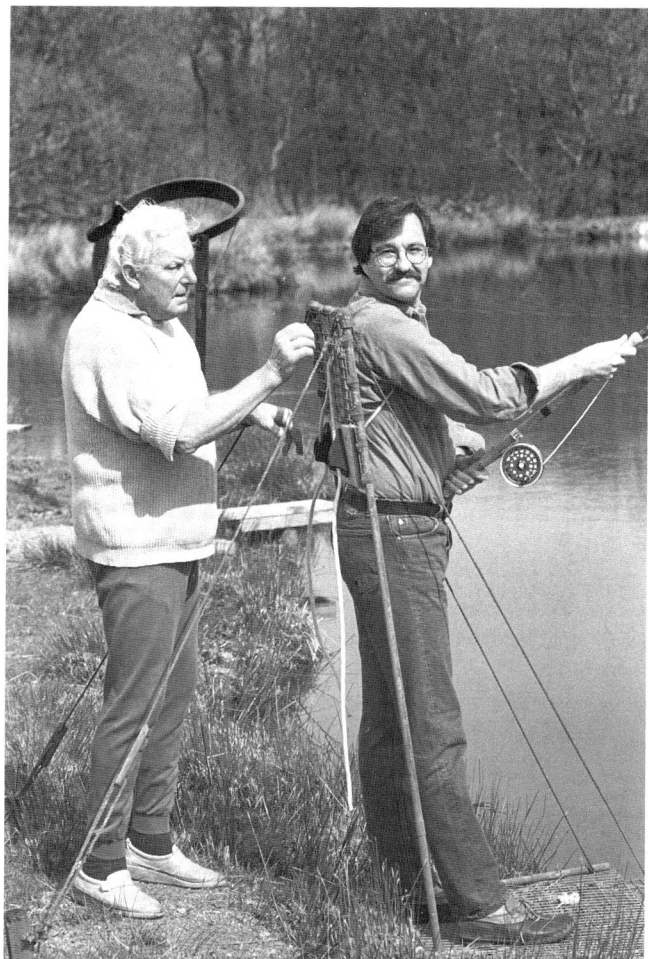

In my early days of instructing I soon realised the impossiblity of making good Speycasters out of people who persisted in behaving like street-corner toys. At my wits' end to know how to cure them, I began to harbour a sadistic longing to nail their shoulders to a cross.

As so often in life when faced with the impractical, I sought a compromise – and after consultation with Bill Arnold, settled for this device, the Crucifix, which is the next best thing.

It has a high success rate.

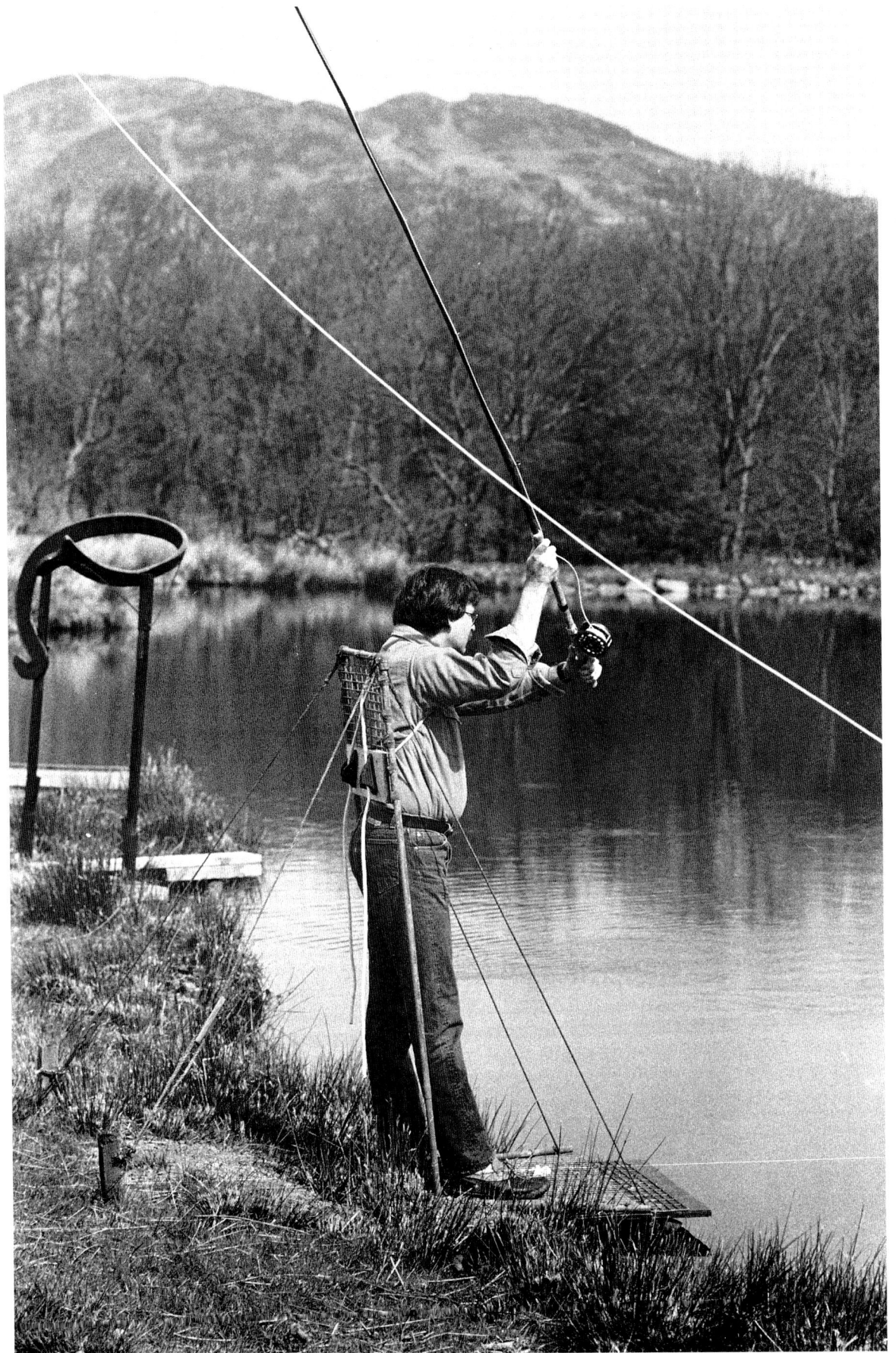

Twenty minutes or so is usually sufficient to show results. The pain of the cords cutting into the shoulder muscles soon convinces the most recalcitrant pupil that all the roll cast needs is the action of forearms and wrists. Already, after ten minutes on the cross, Thomas Pero's casts are showing a marked improvement.

Once all that bobbing body movement and shoulder-rolling is eliminated, we shall be well on the way to making a good roll cast, which will in turn ensure a bravura finish to both single Spey and double Spey casts. To make this as effective and effortless as possible, we must now concentrate on strengthening our wrists. For this we turn to the "Thatcher Stick" …

*The Thatcher Stick*
This eponymous device for strengthening the wrists – more particularly and ironically the *left* wrist – was conceived when the good lady was at the height of her powers. I painted an effigy of her on the target, and my pupils would beat away at it during their "rest" periods.

Naturally, the picture can be painted according to one's political inclinations. In this case it was intended simply as a good natured joke. But with constant beating the Prime Minister's likeness faded and ultimately disappeared, and although in my own mind I feel certain that nothing supernatural was involved, in the light of subsequent events a belief in witchcraft became almost overwhelming.

*Note*: The scene above depicts Thomas Pero beating hell out of the American President.

Stand in the correct roll casting position with feet and hands in their right places and thumbs on top of the rod. As you go through the motions of making a cast, contrive to strike the target a tremendous whack, with both wrists, as the rod reaches eleven o'clock.

After a few minutes' practice using both wrists, take away the right wrist and use only the left. Give it your best shots. This is the really important exercise. Practise often and hard enough and it will lift you right out of the ranks of the also-rans and make you King of the River.

*Left wrist only*
Make a "Thatcher Stick" for yourself. It will work wonders for your wrists, and you will soon notice an improvement in your Speycasting. Any material will suffice, provided it will stand up to a good whacking: a sack of straw; old cushions; a roll of abandoned carpet.

One of my pupils – a famous novelist, keen salmon fisherman and now a splendid Speycaster – was so taken by this idea that he rigged one up in the bedroom of his London flat. "A five minute workout every night at bedtime," he told me, "made a world of difference to my casting. But you should have seen the looks I got from the neighbours!"

## THE MAJOR BELLS

Brooding in the attic one evening about my lack of a Thatcher Stick, and keen to put in some necessary practice, I came upon my daughter's discarded dumb-bells. Pink plastic-sheathed 5-pounders, they lay abandoned on a dusty shelf, having outlived her craze for body-toning and Jane Fonda. Here perhaps was a casting aid more manageable (and less inflammatory) for the married town-dweller than the four-foot rod butt and painted pillow of the original conception. I started with a single weight, moving it above my head to the key positions for Spey and Reverse casts again and again, trying to keep the body balanced and head still. At first, the 5lb weight seemed like a feather, useless for the exercise; but after a few minutes' false-casting, curious cautionary aches and twinges began to reveal muscles that were being tweaked and tested in forearms and elbows. Since it was hurting, I thought, it must be working – a most appropriate conclusion, given the pronouncements of Mrs Thatcher's hapless successor.

The "Major Bells" have become an established daily workout for me. I have persisted in these ten-minute exercises morning and evening for some weeks prior to visiting Tweed. I am sure that considerable benefit in grip, endurance and arm strength is derived from them, not to mention the fun of imagining the line shooting out across the river as one makes the dummy casts. The main incentive now, however, is to develop forearms like John Ashley-Cooper's. I once had lunch with him in an old London club where the bread rolls were notoriously impervious. After inspecting his soup cautiously, the great angler rested a huge hand briefly on his side plate. There was no movement, but a splintering sound and where had once been a granite roll was now a pile of speckled powder. Perhaps he practised with weights, in private.

David Burnett (from a letter)

To help the left thumb stay on duty and do its all important job, I recommend carving a little groove in the butt for the thumb to slide into. This will be found of great benefit, both when fishing and teaching. When necessary, a pupil's thumb can be held in place with a turn of sticky tape.

Here the left thumb slides into the position it will occupy all the time you are casting.

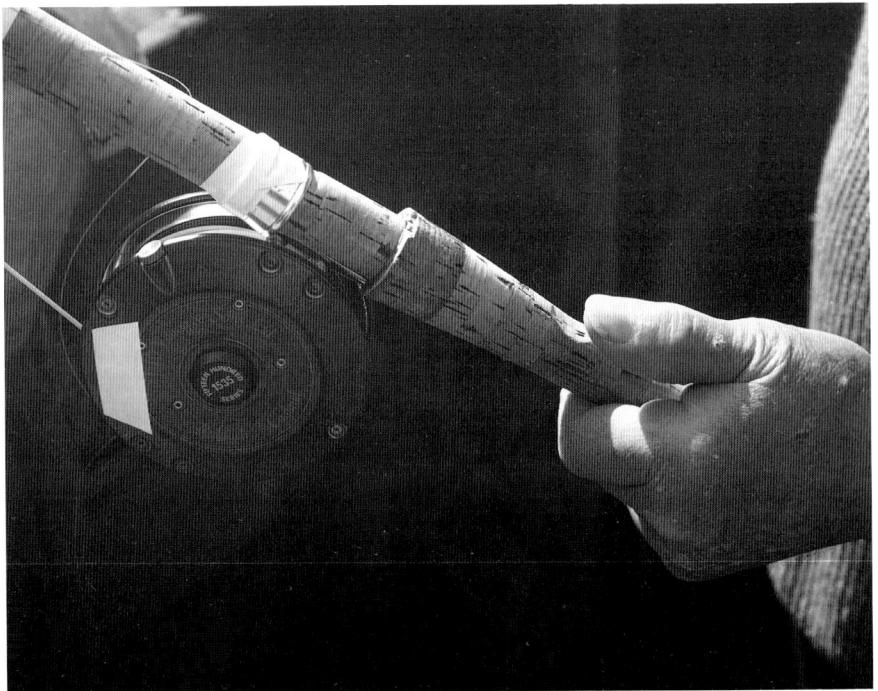

# TRAINING

And now that the rollcasting techniques have been explained, let nothing stop you practising. I don't suppose many of you will take my advice, but there it is. Perhaps in the past you weren't sure of quite what it was you were supposed to be doing, and didn't want to blunder along seeing no sign of improvement. But you haven't that excuse now.

Practise, practise, practise – like the golfer practises. How do you expect to cast a beautiful line if you don't work at it? Just as the golfer spends hours practising his swing; his head and body control; his approach shots; practise your two roll casts. They are the life-blood of all your Speycasting.

Any piece of water will do, either moving or still, so long as enough line can kiss the surface for the "little hands" to grip. I have even taught rollcasting on a small private swimming pool – with the end of the line in the flower beds, but with enough loop on the water for the cast to turn over.

If you think you can dispense with practice you are unique among sportsmen. To practise every day, or even every week may be impossible, but surely you can spare an hour or so every month? To think that you alone among the golfers, cricketers, shooters, javelin-throwers and the like, can cast in the top flight simply by doing nothing whatever for most of the year, is a huge conceit. You sit at your office desks, or whatever, month in month out, and your rods never come out of their cases until you arrive on some salmon river for your fishing holidays. And then you blithely expect to cast like professionals. I know, because I have watched you.

What happens is that you spend much of your precious fishing time working on your neglected casting – and trying to throw the line out of sight. It can't be done.

Just remember this: everything I stress in this book about the importance of head and body control in good casting is no more than the discipline of the scratch golfer – the direct result of practice.

The professional golfer will practise for hours every day, and years ago, when I first began to teach casting for money, so did I.

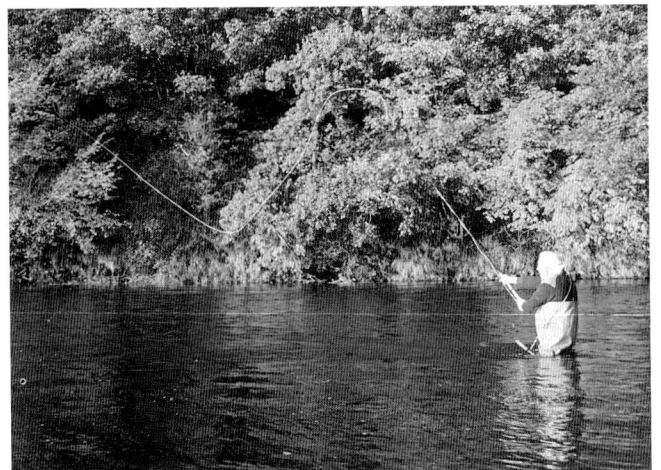

It is on our roll and reverse rollcasting that all our Speycasting depends ...

There is nothing difficult about it. Rollcasting is quite simple. But like the golfer and his swing, we need to practise ...

And go on practising ...

As you experiment there will undoubtedly be a number of poor casts, but don't get disheartened. You will soon find out why a cast goes wrong. Gradually you will get better and better as your wrists strengthen and timing improves.

It is no exaggeration to say that anyone who wants to stay in the top rank as a Speycaster will continue to practise rollcasting for the rest of his or her fishing life.

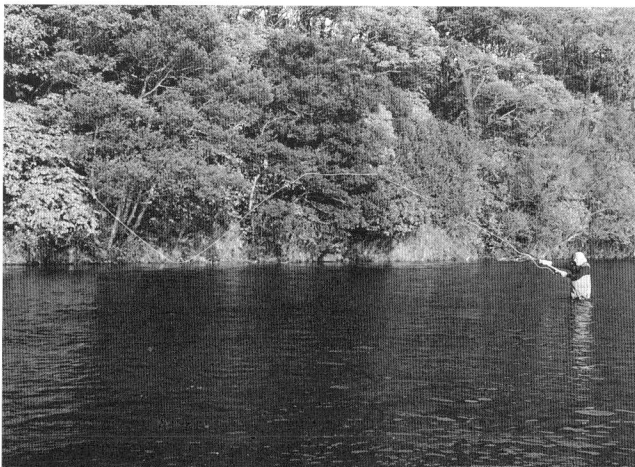

Only by doing so can we hope to come to terms with the fly-caster's greatest enemy – the wind.

You will soon discover that by varying the tilt of the rod in the power-stroke the line can be cast at whatever height you wish ...

Sometimes cutting it out fairly low down to defeat the wind, or – like the cricketer – square-cutting, so that it snakes out underneath branches on the opposite bank ...

Make both roll casts one after the other so that you establish a nice rhythm, swinging the rod from side to side ...

The results indistinguishable one from another. So that when you are fishing, your Spey and reverse Spey will show similar power and accuracy.

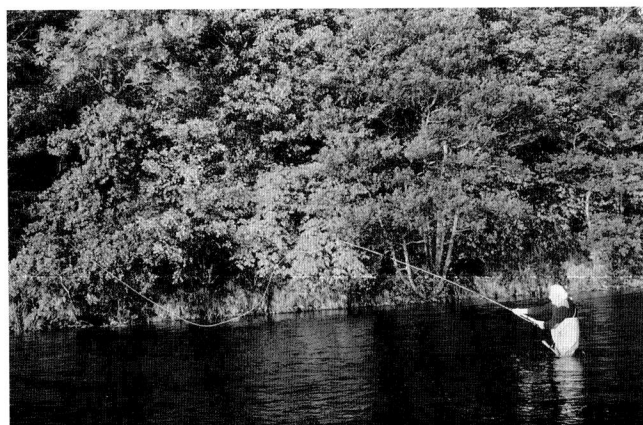

The rule that we should punch our line out *above* the surface so that no disturbance is caused before the fly touches down, is not without exception. There are times when we *want* the belly of the line to land first. In strong winds it is often a help to *anchor the line* so that the water holds it in position while the leader and fly turn over.

The last three pictures in this rollcasting montage illustrate the point. The knack of making this cast will soon come with practice.

It is worth observing that in very windy conditions the surface is usually rippled, thus diminishing the chance of disturbance.

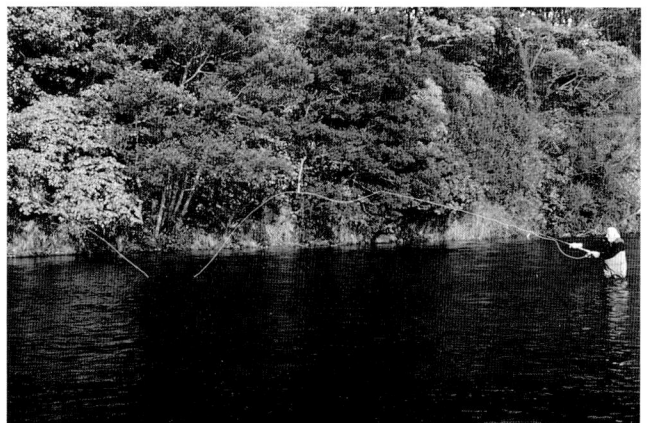

Casting a long belly on the surface.

89

1 Position of feet.

2 Weight on the right leg.

3 Body upright.

4 Rod horizontal.

5 Position of hands (see right-angle triangle) with thumbs on top of butt.

6 Without pulling the line off the water, raise the rod slowly upwards and to the right (left in the case of a reverse cast) in the shape of a crescent moon. Don't rush this stroke, there is no hurry. At the "key" position the rod should be tilted at an angle of 2 o'clock backwards and 2 o'clock sideways.

7 Without any hesitation, *and keeping the rod tilted*, continue a smooth forward movement – accelerating from 2 o'clock to 11 o'clock to form a loop.

8 At 11 o'clock check the rod butt absolutely, by snapping both wrists forward then locking them. The action, as the rod top whips forward, should come right down under your hands. (Try to break the rod!)

9 Aim this power stroke at a point *above* where you want the fly to land to ensure that the line does not hit the water before straightening out.

10 After the power stroke the rod returns to the horizontal, spare line being shot as it does so.

*Note*: Even when casting with a gale behind you, a perfect loop can be formed if, between 2 o'clock and 11 o'clock the rod is kept moving forward faster than the wind speed. (A point to bear in mind when boat fishing.)

Unless you are wading in a moderate current on a firm and level bottom, you will need to position your feet for the Spey cast, *not* the roll cast, when you are rollcasting prior to Spey or double Speycasting. This is to ensure sufficient angle of body-swing during the Spey cast, as described in that chapter.

Unless your footing is assured, to change your stance during a cast is potentially dangerous when wading.

*A Balancing Act* (see picture caption, p.58)
It must be understood that this is as near upright as the author can stand. The turtle-like forward poke of the head is congenital. There is no neck. The skull is plonked straight on to the trunk, like a plasticine man. The glass of liquid will show a slight tilt throughout.

Balancing the glass placed on his cap by cameraman Tony Mottram, the author starts to cast ...

A loop of line is successfully brought back on the water preparatory to the forward shot…

Here comes the power stroke. This is the crunch … but the head has not moved a fraction.

And finally, as the rod returns to the horizontal, the yard or so of spare line rattles out through the rings.

*Note*: This circus act is not part of my normal teaching routine (although, who knows, it may be in future). I did it simply to illustrate what I mean by keeping still and not bobbing about. It is this control of the body that will help to make your casting effortless; improve your accuracy, and certainly increase your casting distance. *Because it is all aimed at making the rod do the work.*

Tell it not in Perth, whisper it not in the streets of Inverness, but nothing better than Scotch Whisky ever came out of Scotland. Only a mentally retarded clown would risk spilling a drop of such life-enhancing spirit. Conceited braggart I may be, but not a fool! If you thought it might have been Scotch in that glass you are very simple-minded. Why risk something so precious on my head when cold tea (a repulsive beverage, drunk by farm workers at the haymaking when I was a boy) would prove the point equally well? And so, cold tea it was, kindly

brewed by my wife Kathleen, who rightly thought such use of Scotch immoral. But I assure you that *this* isn't cold tea. *Cheers*!

And now after all this hilarity we will press on with our Speycasting. First of all the easy ones: the two double Spey casts…

It was a large fish, thick, curved, broad-tailed and all of 20 lb. Very desirable. He was in a high water lie at the tail of the pool under the far bank. That should present no problem, I thought: an overhead cast, a mend, a long slow rolling rise and "Bob's your Uncle", but there was a line of trees behind me! I did everything but place my fly over that salmon, which continued to show. It was all my own fault because I had thought Speycasting unnecessary, a fancy cast not required by a practical down-to-earth fisherman. I never caught the fish, of course, but I made my way rapidly to a casting instructor.

Charles Bingham, *Salmon & Sea Trout Fishing* (1988)

# V   THE DOUBLE SPEY CAST

THIS simple re-directed roll cast is the easiest and safest of all fly casts. It is made from the right bank of the river and, like its counterpart the reverse double Spey cast (which is made from the left bank) is used when a *downstream* wind is blowing.

Having made sure that your feet are in the correct position: right foot slightly forward and pointing in the direction the line is to finish up, weight to be taken on the right leg, start with the rod horizontal and pointing downstream at the fly. Keeping your right arm straight, swing from your hips to the left and bring the rod upstream – low down, not far above the horizontal, so that the line is kept as far away from you as possible. Don't jerk or hurry this stroke. The fly should not leave the water, but glide upstream after the line just as it does during the first half of a roll cast.

When the rod reaches about 135° upstream, raise it in a tiny curl (so that it doesn't actually stop) and bring it straight back again downstream, having described a very shallow figure-of-eight movement. As the rod passes through ninety degrees on its backward journey, a bag of line will be starting to form, and all you have to do now is to make a loop on your right hand side and put out a roll cast across the river at whatever angle you wish.

Breaking the right arm, swing the rod round and up in the crescent curve of a standard roll cast. With both arms rising like pistons, come up to the "key" position – reel well up to if not above your eye-line, rod tilted at 2 o'clock behind and to the right. Now, without the slightest hesitation and propelled by both wrists, the rod moves forward to the power stroke at 11 o'clock. POW! Exactly as in a roll cast, out goes the loop, plucking the fly from its position near the surface downstream and curling it over towards its final touchdown.

At no time during the cast has the fly come anywhere near you. Nothing could be easier. Nothing could be safer.

*Note:* The double Spey is an unhurried, graceful cast, made with an easy rhythm, in one continuous flow with no jerky movements. Remember to keep the rod low down, both when drawing the line upstream and bringing it back downstream. The big swirling loops of line made with an almost vertical rod so beloved of the match-stick men in the old books, are all wrong. You can do what you like in conditions of light air, but in a strong wind you will soon discover your mistake.

Above all, don't rush the forward stroke. As with all Spey casts, *there is no hurry*.

Besides being a very valuable cast in a downstream wind, the double-Spey is absurdly easy to master. So much so that if I find myself taking longer than five minutes to teach someone, I suspect that I am either drunk or dealing with a ninny.

When an Ainu fisherman (from Northern Japan) had brought in his salmon and taken out his hook or spearhead, the fish was far from being dead. To stun it, each man carried a two-foot club of willow wood with which he bashed it over the head. The club had to be made of willow, and not of any other kind of wood or of stone because, according to the Ainu creation myth, the backbone of the first man was made of willow, and they therefore considered it the noblest kind of wood. They believed that, if struck with any other kind of club, the fish would not run the following year.

Carleton S. Coon, *The Hunting Peoples* (1971)

Start of the double Spey cast. Angler wading downstream under densely wooded right bank which makes overhead casting impossible. After the previous cast the fly has swung round across the current and finished up straight downstream at the dangle. To make a new cast, the object is to gain sufficient slack line to form a loop that can be roll cast across the river at whatever angle is desired.

Holding his right arm straight and his body upright the angler swings round from his hips to the left, keeping the line as far away from his legs as possible *by holding the rod point low down*. (The reason for this is to ensure that when he comes to make the loop for his roll cast, there will be sufficient line kissing the water for the "little hands" to grab.)

Following the rod, line, leader and fly come gliding upstream along the surface.

At the end of the swing (about 135° upstream) the rod is kept moving by means of a slight upwards tilt which, as the rod is brought back downstream, forms a shallow figure-of-eight.

Now a bag of line has started to form as the rod is swept round and up towards the "key" position of the roll cast.

With the rod tilted slightly to the side, as in all roll and Spey casts, the loop is punched out across the river, taking with it the leader and fly.

No fly cast is easier to perform than this. It is just a simple re-directed roll cast, and when made in a downstream wind as it always should be, there is nothing safer.

You watch your mentor delivering his cast; the long serpentine curve straightens over the water; a little tilt of the butt, and the casting line, though the lightest part of the projectile, falls not first, but furthest; nothing can be more graceful and, at the same time, appear so easy. You take the rod and try to do the same. Your perceptor's movements were noiseless – how is it that when you imitate them the rod makes a loud "swoosh" through the air? How is it that instead of flying out far and fair the line either falls on the water in what a good old gillie of mine used to call a "burble", or, at most, scrambles out in a wriggling, uncertain manner, depositing the fly half-a-dozen yards away from the spot aimed at?

Sir Herbert Maxwell: *Salmon & Sea Trout* (1898)

# VI   THE REVERSE DOUBLE SPEY CAST

THE reverse double Spey cast is made from the left bank of the river. Like its counterpart discussed in the last chapter, it is simply a re-directed roll cast, only this time in reverse. You can, of course, ignore reverse casting and work entirely from the other shoulder, putting the left hand up the rod and casting from the left leg instead of from the right. And most people fish like this. But as I have already suggested, sooner or later you will find an inability to reverse cast a great disadvantage. In fact there are times when you are going to feel seriously deprived. This will soon become obvious when you find yourself fishing from the left bank with a sinking line – or indeed with any sort of line on water that demands a roll cast preparatory to the main thrust.

A moment's thought will put this into perspective. Imagine you are standing on the left bank in a strong downstream wind, faced with the prospect of making a roll cast – either to bring your line and fly to the surface, or to straighten the line from a back-eddy. If there are bushes or other obstructions on the bank you can only roll cast back downstream from the right shoulder. What are you going to do then, if unable to reverse double Spey cast?

If you wish, you can work from the other shoulder and start with a reverse roll cast, in which case it will be followed by a normal double Spey cast. But it must be one technique or the other. You cannot have it both ways.

In short, if you wish to be a complete Speycaster, you must be able to make all the casts described in this book off either shoulder, and those of course include the reverse casts.

Another occasion when we soon recognise the advantages of reverse casting is when we are fishing in what I call a "headstrong" wind – that is, a strong wind constantly changing a hundred-and-eighty degrees in direction. Many river valleys act rather like wind tunnels. On water that flows between high banks or cliffs, a wind that is gusting at gale force upstream one minute may be gusting straight downstream the next. On a pool which friends and I fish regularly, a high wind frequently behaves like this, blowing hard upstream for a cast or two, then switching suddenly and sending a hearty blast downstream. We have no trouble with it, simply reading the wind on face or neck as we wade the pool and, without changing feet or hands, go straight into a single Spey cast or a reverse double Spey cast according to the changes in wind direction. In those conditions, anyone unable to reverse cast would find that pool extremely difficult if not impossible to fish.

Once the use of the left wrist has become second nature in the reverse roll cast, reverse double Speycasting is simple enough. Like casting from the other bank, you are just setting yourself up with a loop of line to roll out over the river. There is, however, a little trick which makes it all that much easier.

Swing from the hips to the right as you bring the rod upstream, and swing back with it to the left, *then* as you raise the

Angler casting from the left side of the river. Starts with line and fly straight downstream. Then swings upstream to the right, keeping the rod low and the right arm extended ...

rod towards the reverse "key" position *make a little half-swing back to the right*. This helps to put the rod beautifully into place, with your right hand straight up above your head. Now all that remains to be done is to keep the rod tilted to the left and make the forward stroke.

Well executed, the reverse double Spey is a very powerful cast and I find I can throw a longer and more accurate line with it than by changing over and casting left-handed. You may well find it awkward at first – like all reverse casting it needs practice – but hang on to it. Don't try to cast too long a line to start with. Be patient and persevere. The rewards are golden.

Upstream to an angle of about 135° ...

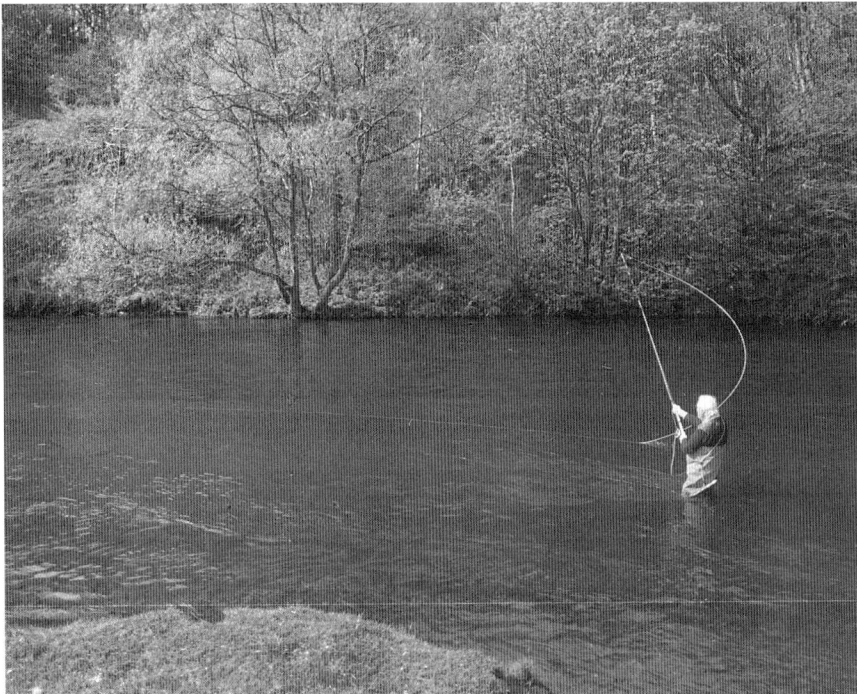

He makes a slight upward curl of the rod, to prevent it from coming to a halt, and describes a shallow figure-of-eight curve in the line as he starts to bring the rod back downstream.

The fly and leader have followed the line upriver and are now waiting out of harm's way downstream as the rod swings back ...

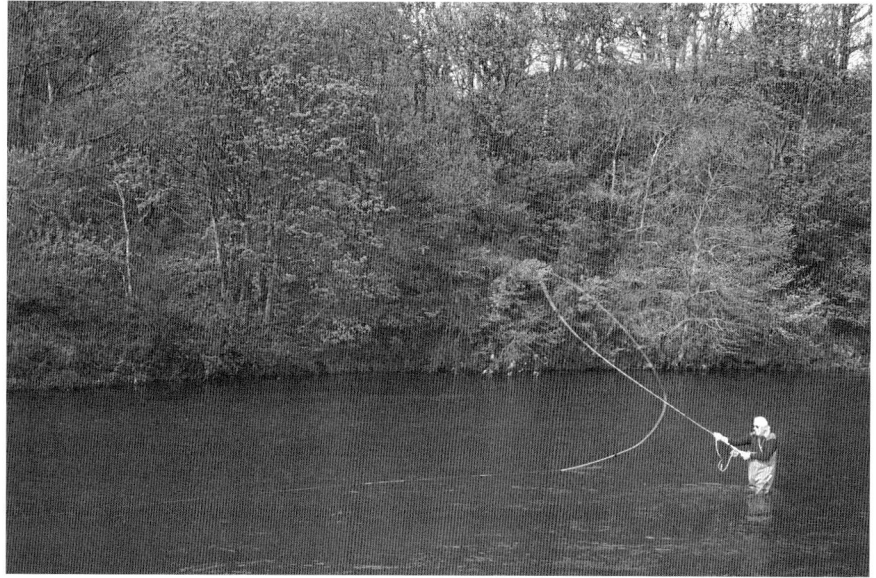

Now, as the rod continues on its way round to the left and starts to climb into the "key" reverse position ...

A loop of line is beginning to form.

Here the loop is ready to be punched out, with the rod high in the full "key' position. *Note*: It is tilted safely to the left. And that is where it will remain.

The reverse roll cast in action. The movement immediately following the power stroke. The loop of line has started to roll out over the water, picking up leader and fly from downstream – where they have been kept safely out of the way.

*Note*: After the power stroke, as the rod returns to the horizontal, the angler's right forefinger drops like a released safety-catch, removing the tension, so that the slack line goes rattling out through the rod rings as the friction between line and rings becomes minimal.

Finally, the loop stretches out over the river taking with it the slack line shot on the forward stroke. A powerful and accurate cast.

*Note*: In the same way that the double Spey cast is designed for fishing from the *right* bank in a *downstream wind*, the reverse double Spey is the cast for use on the *left* bank.

In windless conditions or very light airs you can please yourself whether you make a single Spey or a reverse double Spey, but *never try to make a reverse double Spey cast in a strong upstream wind*.

Remember this: If you misuse Speycasting in strong winds, it can become potentially as dangerous as overhead casting.

For upstream winds we need the single Spey cast, the subject of our next chapter.

The Island Pool, so called from a small piece of land which at a certain height of the river is neither submerged nor attached to the mainland, is situated between two spurs of opposite hills, and on my arrival was being whipped into cream by the fury of the gale. To attempt an overhead cast in such a wind, and in full view of an observant and critical ghillie, was too much of a risk, and so I decided to show him one of my best Spey-casts. Faithfully I carried out all the instructions . . . I coaxed the fly into position, switched back the loop with a movement which was nothing if not rhythmic, and hurried it forward. With a resounding smack the fly buried itself in my leg. And that was that; ghillie or no ghillie there was no pretending anything else.

Gingerly I cut the cast, removed as much as possible of the gaudy dressing from the fly and as little as could be of the less gaudy dressing from myself, and surveyed the damage. My oilskin and thick tweed suit had fortunately prevented the barb from biting as deeply into my leg as might otherwise have been the case.

"It will come oot wi' a pull," remarked the ghillie, who hitherto had been content to remain a silent spectator, and, without so much as a by your leave, administered a tug which left the hook with no alternative but to let go. Handing me back the blood-soaked remains of the fly he recommended that I should adopt a different method of casting.

Robert Hartman: *About Fishing* (1935)

# VII  THE SINGLE SPEY CAST

## 1  TRADITIONAL

This is not intended as a book on salmon fly-fishing tactics, but perhaps a word or two on the *purpose* of a cast may not be out of place. First, as intimated in the Introduction, I would like to expand on the use of the Traditional Spey cast – or what I call "lazy man's" fishing. It is a very simple and relaxed way of fishing down (or backing up) a pool, and this is the way I go about it.

After the fly has swung across the pool and comes towards the dangle, I draw in line to keep the fly moving through the slacker water, and continue to keep it on the move by raising the rod with a 2 o'clock outward tilt. Then, with the arms at full stretch, I swing from the hips and sweep the rod in a shallow "U" curve upstream. (The "Underhand Throw" as mentioned by most of the old writers.)

The fly leaves the water and, following the line in a parabolic curve, pitches just upstream of my right shoulder. The rod meanwhile has swung round and up towards the (by now familiar) "key" position, and is continuing forward in a roll cast at whatever angle I have determined, accelerating to the position of 11 o'clock whereupon the butt is checked solidly in the "power stroke".

The remainder of the manoeuvre is simply the completion of the roll cast: the loop extending over the water, while the rod comes down to the horizontal. All slack line accumulated during the fly's final stages of its passage across the pool being shot as the angle between rod and water lessens – that is, as the friction between line and rod-rings diminishes.

Ignoring the advice generally given by the pundits about moving between casts, it is now that I shuffle downstream. Not always with floating line, though quite often, but *always* (if possible) with sinking line – as described in Chapter IX.

The advantage of moving downstream the moment a cast is made, not *between* casts, is surely obvious. It avoids disruption. It enables the fly to be kept fishing much longer and greatly increases the chance of hooking a salmon that has followed the fly for the last yard or two of its swing close to and across the dangle – a popular taking place. That fish behave like this quite frequently in some pools, I know, for I have watched them. And caught them too. (Our move downstream between casts when fishing the deep sunk fly is mainly for an entirely different reason, but we shall be dealing with that in Chapter IX.) Generally speaking, the only sensible time to move *between* casts is when we are *backing up* a pool.

The traditional technique of Speycasting is ideal for this kind of "lazy man's" fishing with a floating line. All one has to do at the completion of a cast is to raise the rod and, without any hiatus, put out a new cast. Then move downstream. It is a very restful, easy, rhythmical way of fishing a pool, and the "Underhand throw" is ideally suited to it.

But when we come to make the figure-of-eight Spey cast, for which the Casting Simulator is designed, we need to work from a different story-line.

## 2  FIGURE-OF-EIGHT

First of all, as mentioned earlier, the traditional technique is fiendishly tricky to teach. Very useful once it has been conquered but difficult to learn. Simply because one cannot *teach how hard to pull the fly* in the "U"-shaped underhand upstream throw. It can only be *demonstrated*. People have to pick it up as best they can by trial and error, and as I know from my experience of the last ten or twelve years, many fall by the wayside. By comparison, the figure-of-eight Speycast is easily taught, and quite quickly, too. Apropos of which, I have noticed something rather curious: that once a pupil has mastered the figure-of-eight cast, as often as not he gets hold of the traditional throw quite quickly. This is one reason why I concentrate first and foremost on the figure-of-eight technique.

Another reason, as we shall see later, is that the figure-of-eight pick-up is much more efficient than the traditional cast when we are fishing a quick-sinking line.

I have claimed that the figure-of-eight is easily learnt, and so it is, but only if certain conditions are observed – in particular the position of the feet. It is when we come to make this cast that we begin to understand the importance of footwork. Unless we get our feet in the correct position: right foot pointing across the river in the direction our fly is to travel, left foot at a comfortable forty-five degrees, we cannot swing our body round from the hips far enough to the right while making the first half of the cast. This movement is essential if the cast is to become automatic. (A cricketer or game-shooter will grasp the point immediately.)

What you *must* be able to do when learning this cast is to swing around in advance of the rod and *look at the spot on the water forty-five degrees upstream of your right shoulder where you want to place the fly.*

Whatever you choose to do later in life, when casting has become second nature, it is imperative that you make this movement when *learning*. Failure to do so will result almost invariably in the fly finishing up short of its true position and will make mastery of this otherwise simple cast extremely difficult.

In my experience, the major fault of most beginners who have difficulty in acquiring the Spey cast, lies nearly always in the position of their feet. In this, fly-casters are not alone . . .

Visiting a famous Fleet Street bar one lunch-time long ago, I had the honour and good fortune to drink a glass of wine with one of the greatest batsmen in the history of cricket, a boyhood hero of mine, Jack Hobbs.

"Forgive me for talking shop", I said during our chat. "But as a very keen cricketer may I ask you one question about batsmanship?"

"Of course," he nodded. "Go ahead."

"In your opinion, sir," I asked. "What is the most important point for a batsman to remember?"

The great man looked at me and smiled.

"Footwork," he said simply. "Footwork."

And if you were to ask me the same question with regard to Speycasting, I would give you the same answer.

The skilled execution of so many human physical activities depends on footwork, and Speycasting is no exception. The first thing to think about when preparing to make a cast is the position of your feet. *Point your right foot where you want the cast to go*. Do that and you are nearly home. If you have learnt and practised the correct figure-of-eight rod movement, the rest of the cast is automatic.

Forget about the fly. Forget about the line. Once you have placed your feet and started the figure-of-eight curve, swing from your hips ahead of the rod and look at the water forty-five degrees upstream of your right shoulder – and the fly will land where you are looking. *Every time.*

This is not mumbo-jumbo. I am not a witch doctor. It is a plain statement of fact. To do what I tell you for the first time when you are learning, demands faith. And that is exactly what I din into my pupils when they are working on the casting simulator. "Have faith in what I say. Point your right foot. Swing from the hips as the rod comes round. Look at that patch of water where you want the fly to land and it will land there. It is all automatic. You don't have to use any force. You don't have to pull it."

After that it is simply the completion of a roll cast – which, after all, is what you have set yourself up to make. By the time the fly has touched down upstream, the rod is on its upward journey towards the "key" position. Without the slightest pause, sweep it round and forward to its climax at 11 o'clock. And then, with both wrists, WOW – and out it goes.

*Finish of two Spey casts*
Note the position of the hands at the completion of both casts. There is no hint of the left hand being dragged backwards, it has done its full share of the work and helped to keep the line well clear of the water. Notice also the upright stance, the weight being taken on the right leg.

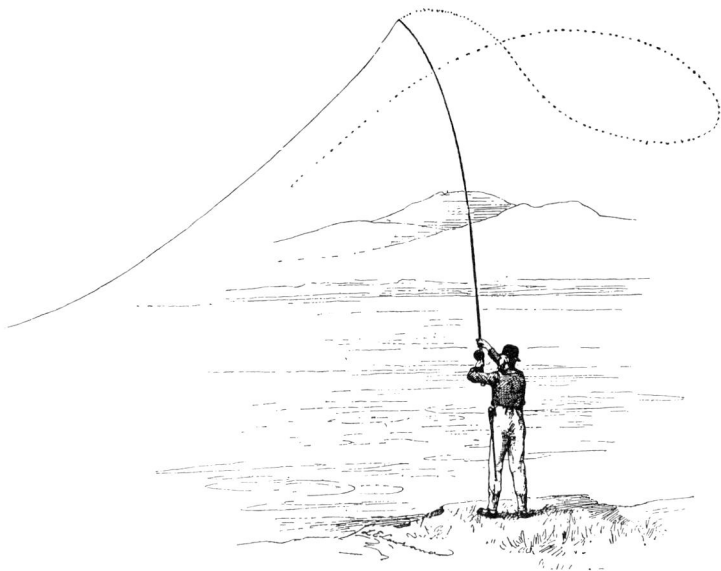

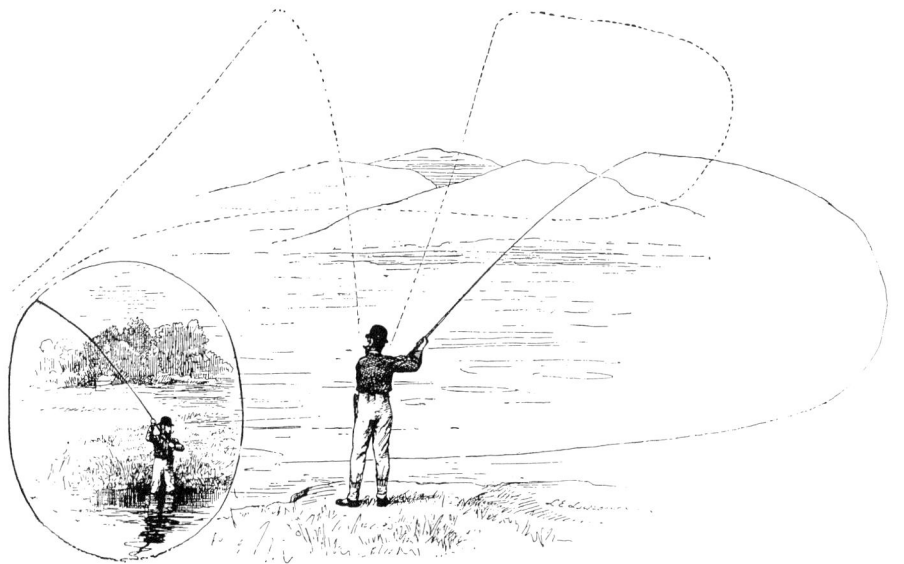

George Kelson, demonstrating The Spey Cast (or Underhand Throw). From his book *The Salmon Fly*: How to Dress it and How to Use it (1895).

Apart from a rather bizarre grip on the rod, an unusual hat and casting off the wrong leg – which wouldn't have done his back much good – George is making a fair attempt at it. At least we can understand what he is trying to do, which is more than can be said for some of the illustrations offered by his contemporaries. But what he has to say about it doesn't take us much further forward.

> The reader is now sufficiently at home with various systems of casting to have formed for himself one particular conclusion, as most Fishermen would. What is this one particular conclusion?
>
> That the achievement of any individual cast is an art, and from the very nature of it, the achievement of the much-coveted "Spey," the highest art of all – is an art endowed with an irresistible fascination peculiar to itself and so enjoyable that I may leave it without further comment. But in truth, the "Spey" is to fishing what words are to thoughts, for without it certain waters cannot be commanded, and without words certain thoughts cannot be expressed. To sum up. What is the chief end of the system?
>
> The "Spey" system's chief end may be briefly put thus: – That men who are practically conversant with all the circumstances which render the cast necessary, and with all the various ways of making it, are so far removed from the struggling rank and file, as to frequently meet with the highest success on pools which, to others, are positively unfishable.

The 1930s showed no advance on Kelson. Here are some notes about it together with some drawings from *Salmon Fishing* (1931) Eric Taverner *et al.*

The Spey-cast is really the same as a switch done sideways . . .

In each method the function of the left hand is for the most part to steady the rod, while the right hand does the larger share of the work of propulsion.

This is the way to make a plain switch: although everyone at times adapts the cast to fit the circumstances and therefore employs the hundred and one different variations that exist between the ortho-dox switch and the Spey-cast. The rod point is lowered, until the line is held taut by the current, is then raised to the vertical and allowed to go a little beyond it and slightly to right or stream-side of you. The line will follow the point back in a deeply-sagging belly and the fly will remain in the water, but near the surface. The rod is then brought forward and slightly outwards, so that the backward and for-ward paths of the line cross at an acute angle; and, if the rhythm has been maintained, there should be no risk of two parts of the line get-ting foul of one another. The line near the tip of the rod, on going forward, will do so in a roll, will pick up the remainder of the line and will impart to it impetus enough to cause it to extend itself in the new direction.

The essential to success is an absence of pause from beginning to end, save for one instant just before the rod comes forward. The rhythm is necessarily accented, because there should be slight accel-eration on the upward path and a decided finish to the forward stroke . . .

With a two-handed rod, you can, if you wish, keep the leading hand quite low; and the rod point may also be taken back along a lowered path, if branches or the arch of a bridge make it impossible for the rod to be lifted vertically . . . There are endless ways of pre-senting a fly to a fish, or rather the ways are only limited in number by the amount of ingenuity displayed by the angler in overcoming difficulties. And that is more than half the joy of fishing . . .

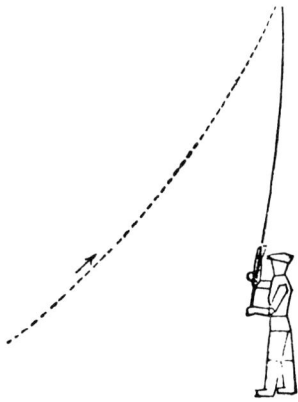

Fig. 47.
READY TO BEGIN THE SWITCH.

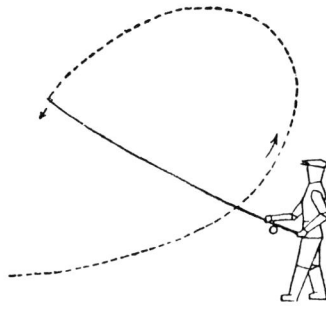

Fig. 48.
HALF-WAY THROUGH THE DOWN-
WARD CUT.

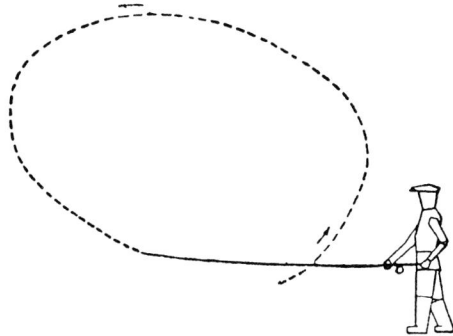

The drawings illustrate some of the
more obvious casting faults of old
that have persisted to the present
time. Compare the similarity of
this cast with the roll cast on p.48.

THE FINISH OF THE SWITCH.

Fig. 49

If this chap continues to cast with a
vertical rod and his line as close as
it is, he will be lucky to avoid
hooking himself before the day is
out.

Fig. 50.
THE SINGLE SPEY
The line extended downstream.

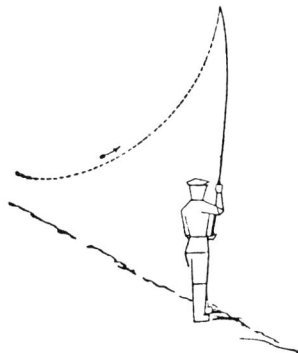

Fig. 51.
THE SINGLE SPEY.
The rod in the vertical position.

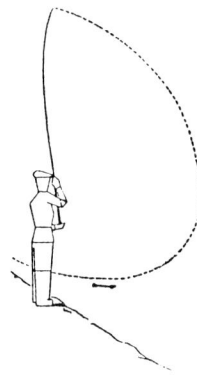

Fig. 52.
THE SINGLE SPEY.
The line travelling upstream.

Fig. 53.
THE SINGLE SPEY.
The downward finish.

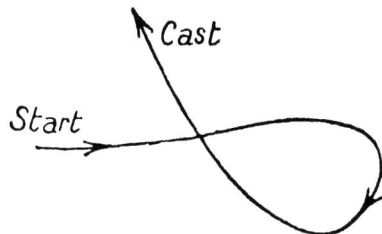

THE SINGLE SPEY.
The track of the rod-point seen from above.

Fig. 54.

115

And here for good measure is a double Spey cast made from the left shoulder off the left bank. It has a familiar list of faults: belly-casting off the wrong leg; holding the rod like a broom-stick; Using the bottom hand as a pivot; failing to tilt the rod, and so allowing the line to come too close; holding the arms too low; not swinging from the hips. Does this fellow get *any* marks? Yes – for standing upright and not body-bobbing. (But for all that, he will finish up with a sore back!)

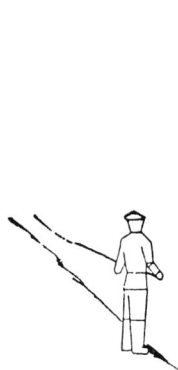

**Fig. 55.**

The line extended down-stream.

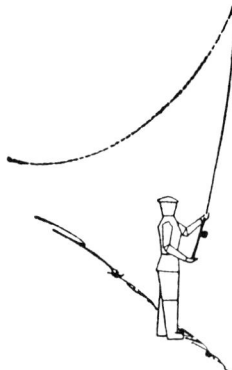

**Fig. 56.**

The rod coming to the vertical. The line following upstream.

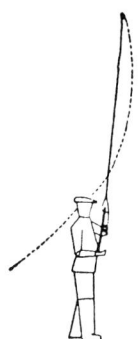

**Fig. 57.**

The rod vertical. The line travelling upstream.

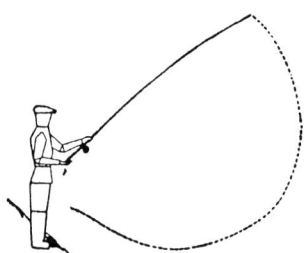

**Fig. 58.**

The rod over the stream but about to come back. The line still travelling upstream.

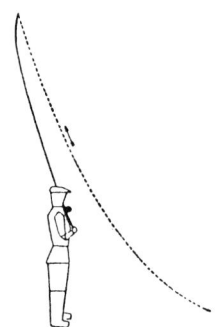

**Fig. 59.**

The rod back over the bank. The line following it.

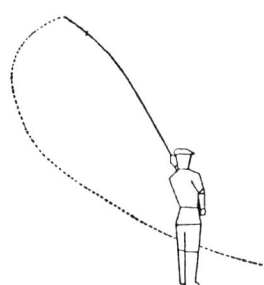

**Fig. 60.**

The line coming back under the rod which is at the extreme left of the circular movement.

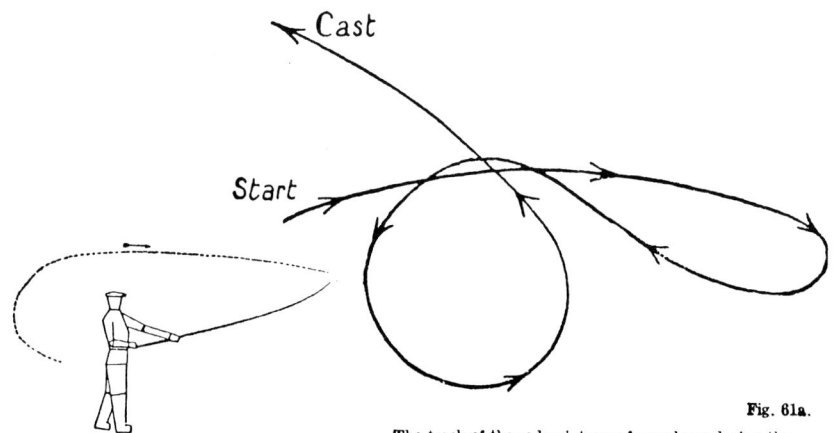

**Fig. 61.**

The final cast in the direction required.

**Fig. 61a.**

The track of the rod-point seen from above during the double Spey-cast.

**THE DOUBLE SPEY-CAST.**

116

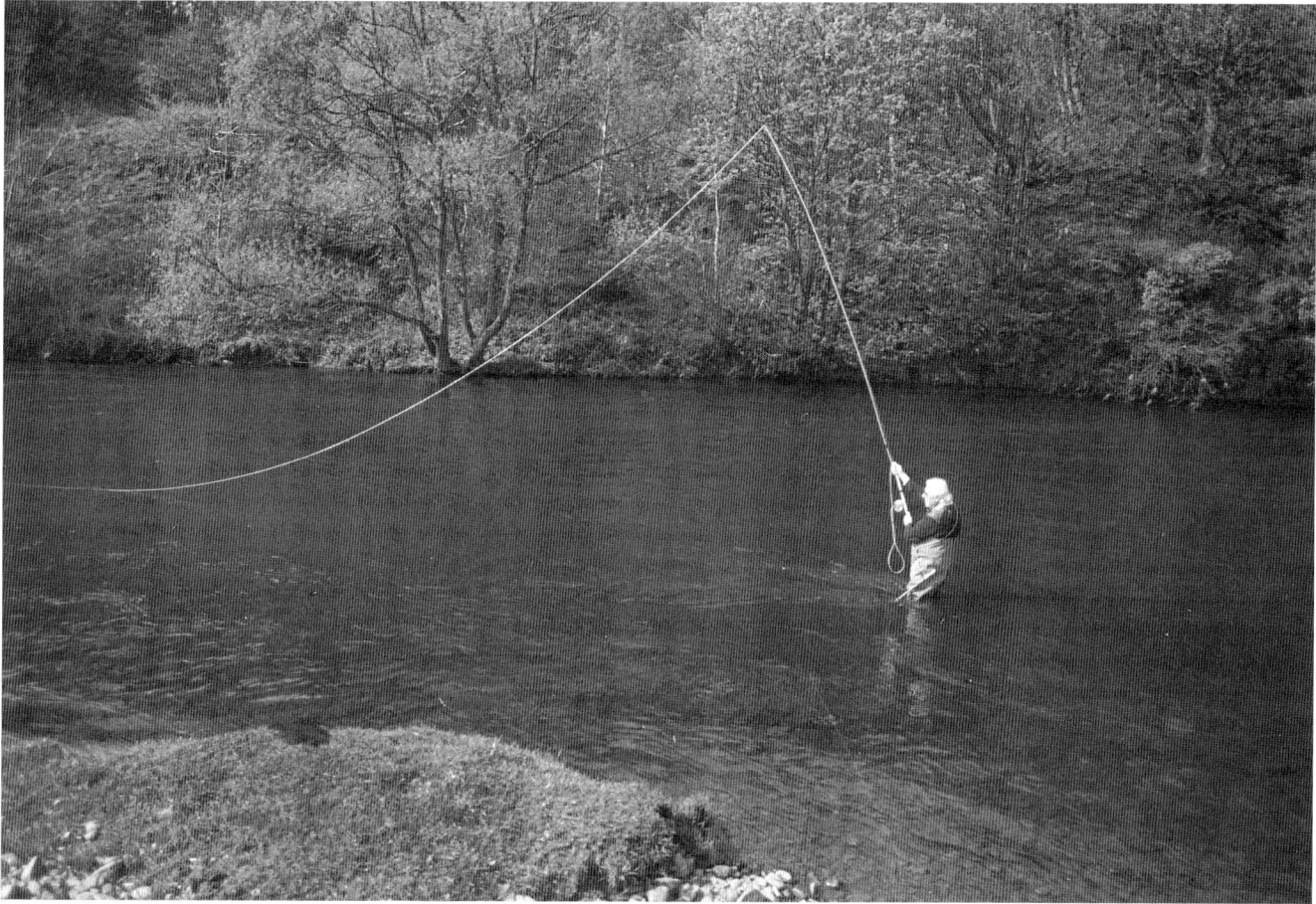

*The traditional Spey or "Underhand" throw.*
Tilting the rod outwards, to keep the line clear on its upstream journey, the angler raises it with arms at full stretch.

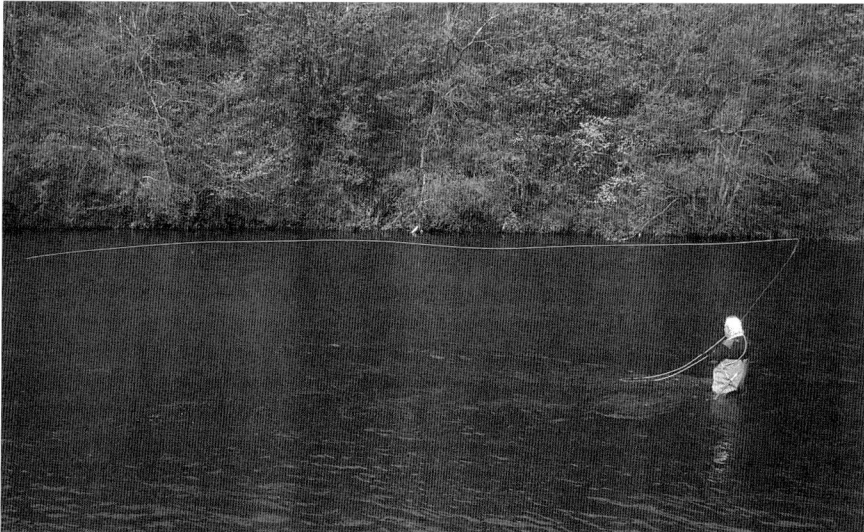

Dipping the rod point towards the opposite bank, he swings the rod upriver bringing the line after it in a shallow parabola.

The fly lands out in the current a yard or two upstream of the angler's right shoulder (far enough to compensate for the current and to avoid line and fly being swept past him before he has had time to complete the forward stroke).

Here, having been brought up through the "key" position, the rod is in the final stage of the roll cast that has punched the fly outwards at an angle downstream.

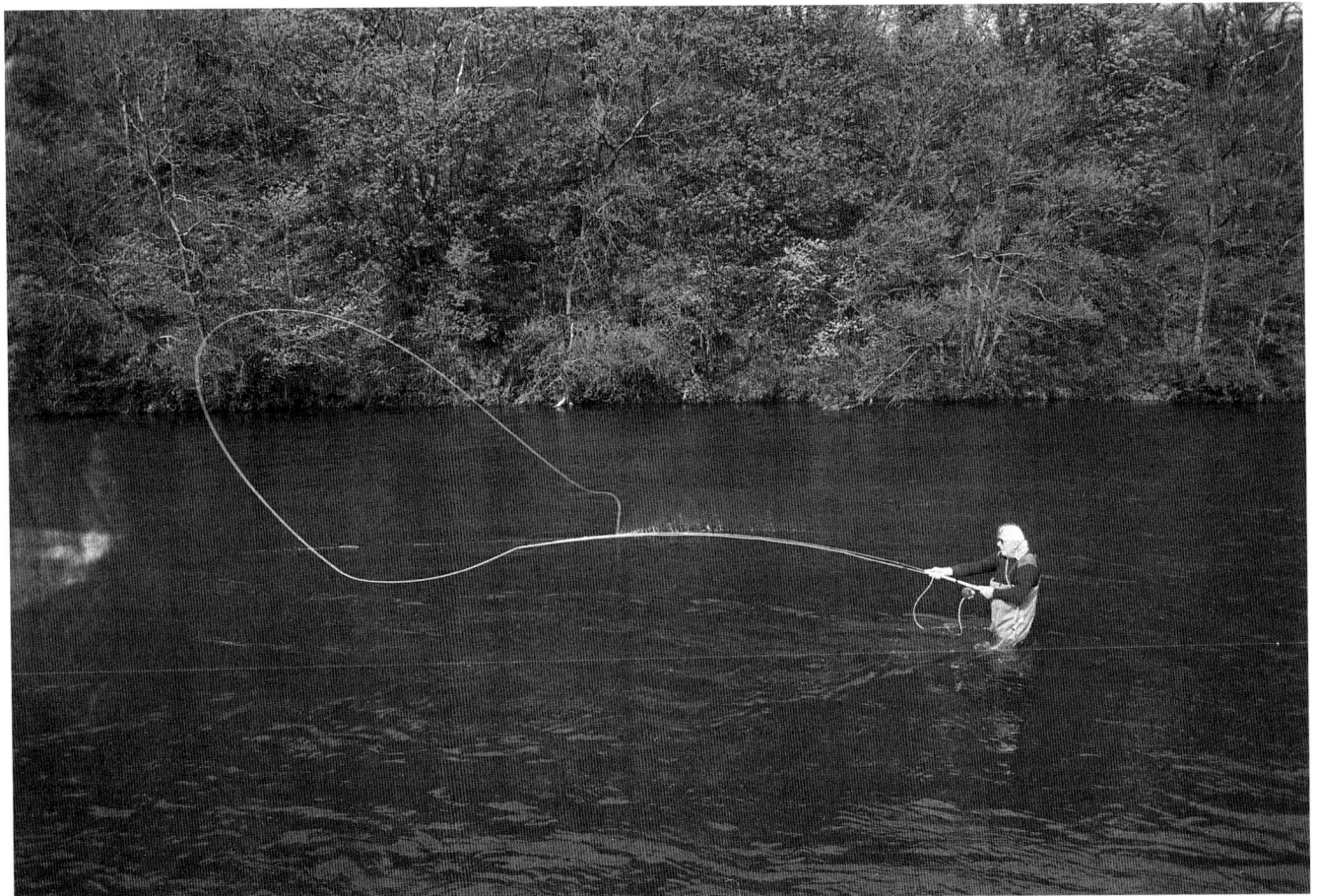

*"Lazy man's fishing"*
At the end of a cast the fly has come to the dangle straight downstream. To keep it on the move in case a salmon has followed it, the angler stays where he is and draws in some line ...

Now, from the same position, both to maintain upstream movement on the fly and to make the first stroke of the traditional Spey cast, the angler raises the rod and switches the fly upstream with a "U" shaped curve of the rod (or "underhand throw"), pitching the fly ...

... just upstream of his right shoulder. *Note*: Until making this move he has been in with a chance of hooking a fish. Still in the same position he completes his Spey cast, keeping the rod tilted to the right and aiming his loop at an angle downstream and across ...

The line goes snaking out across the river ...

... and straightens above the water, taking with it the slack line stripped in at the finish of the previous cast. It is now that the angler makes his downstream shuffle – compensating if necessary for any unnatural fly behaviour by movement of the rod.

From the angling literature throughout the ages which has come my way, the writer who has seemed to me to come closest to what I think and teach about Speycasting is John Bickerdyke in *The Book of the All-Round Angler* (1888).

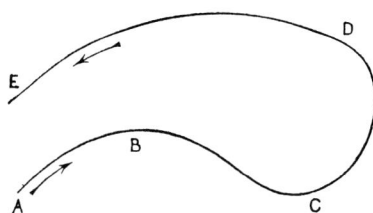

FIG. 27.  CURVE FOLLOWED BY ROD-POINT
IN SPEY OR SWITCH CAST.

The Spey cast is particularly useful where, owing to trees or a high bank, the line cannot be extended at all behind the angler . . .

It is not a difficult cast to understand, and I would beg of my young readers to master it, for it is at times most useful . . . We are looking down the river, let us say, with a high rock behind us. Our rod point is rather low, pointing towards the fly, and our line is, of course, extended downstream. Suppose, now, our rod-point is at A (see Fig. 27); we raise it smartly, following the curve shown, to B, when our line will be off the water; then we depress it again to C, and raise it to D, by which time the fly and a portion of the line will be touching the water almost at our feet; then we switch the rod forward sharply from D to E, and the line follows round in a curve, leaves the water, and rolls out down stream in front of us. The progress of the rod-point from A to D must be steady, and rather quick than slow; but from D to E it can hardly be too quick.

Bickerdyke seems to have got at least halfway towards achieving the figure-of-eight cast I teach. The diagram of his rod movement is certainly reminiscent of the Speycasting Simulator. Which takes us logically in that direction . . .

A figure-of-eight Spey cast made on the Simulator Mk II with full rod and line.

The line has been laid out on the water straight "downstream" to the angler's left, with the rod pointing at the fly. From there the rod has been swung round the ascending figure-of-eight curve of the Simulator at an angle of about forty-five degrees. As it passes a position at right-angles to the water, the line and fly are drawn clear of the surface. Then, as the rod follows the downward curve (as it is doing here) the line will come streaking "upstream" in a low parabola ...

... leading the fly down into exactly the right place on the surface, while the rod, travelling along the continuing upward curve, is automatically swinging round towards the "key" position of the final roll cast ...

After which, all that remains to be done is to punch out the big loop that has formed in front of and to the right-hand side of the angler. The rod is checked in the power stroke at 11 o'clock (before it hits the rim of the Simulator) and …

… away goes the line, taking the yard or two of slack with it and rolling out well up in the air over the water. For once the rod stays where it is, being unable to drop any lower.

From start to finish the cast has been entirely automatic. Note the position of the feet; right foot slightly ahead of the left foot and pointing in the direction of the forward stroke – thus enabling the angler to swing easily into position.

In close-up we can see stage by stage how the Simulator works. These are posed pictures showing the various rod positions but without the verisimilitude of a taut line.

First of all the rod is horizontal and pointing along the line at the fly and seated in its little crook on the left side of the Simulator. As it starts its figure-of-eight movement, *it curls to the left ...*

... in a climbing curve that changes direction and carries on round to the right. In doing so it picks up the line and turns it over, so that it no longer points straight downstream but at a slight angle away from the bank. (It is along this new angle that line and fly will travel.)

The rod moves round the Simulator rim at a maximum angle of about forty-five degrees' outward tilt, thus keeping the line well clear of the bank. As the rod reaches a position at right-angles to the bank, the fly leaves the water and starts to follow the line upstream along its new path.

124

Here, maintaining the exact curve of the Simulator rim, the rod has dipped down and then started to rise again. The fly meanwhile is just pitching on the surface, out from the bank and to the angler's right ...

The final lift of the Simulator's rim has sent the rod up in the air on its way to the "key" position. A loop is forming away from the bank and slightly to the angler's right – and all that remains is to make the power stroke that will punch it out over the water.

The Simulator has greatly simplified instruction. After practising on it long enough to burn the figure-of-eight pattern of rod movement on the brain, most pupils can put out a workable Spey cast straightaway – although few have ever done anything like it before.

## LINE JERKING

A very common mistake is to *rush* the end of a Spey cast – whether single or double – by bringing the rod up at an abrupt angle in a straight line, instead of swinging it round and up in a crescent-moon curve. This jerks the line off the water and destroys the loop. A good loop is essential to all roll and Spey casting. Without it, a cast is doomed.

REMEMBER: Speycasting consists of a series of curves. Apart from the power-strokes, *there are no straight lines*.

*Figure-of-eight Spey cast*
The rod has moved to the left from the horizontal and is now climbing round to the right, rising to a maximum angle of about forty-five degrees. *Note*: The rod is kept tilted throughout the cast. At no time does it come to the vertical.

When the rod is just approaching a right-angle to the bank, the line and fly leave the water at the start of their low airborne path upstream ...

The angler has swung round and is placing the fly upstream of his right shoulder. Meanwhile the rod, having dipped down (to help place the fly), has started its swing round and up towards the "key" position.

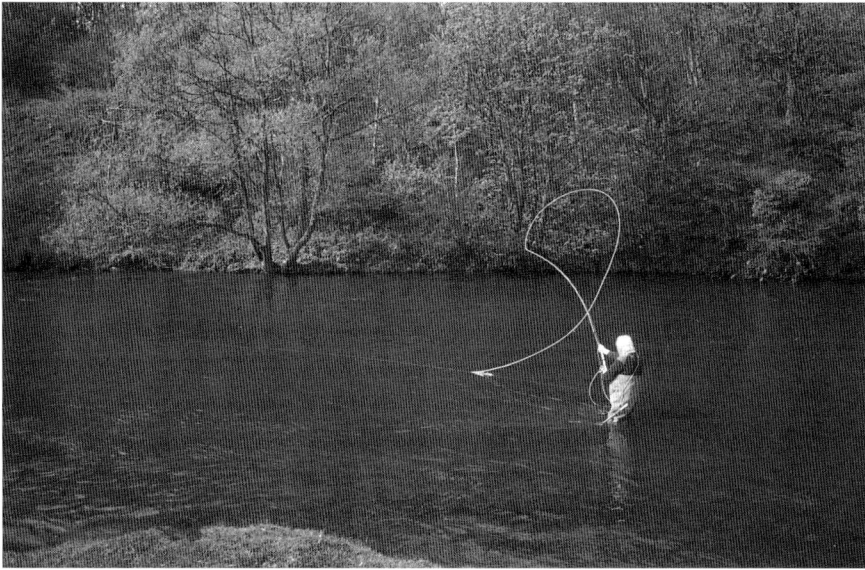

All the angler has done so far is simply to set himself up to make this re-directed roll cast ...

And away goes the loop, picking up leader and fly ...

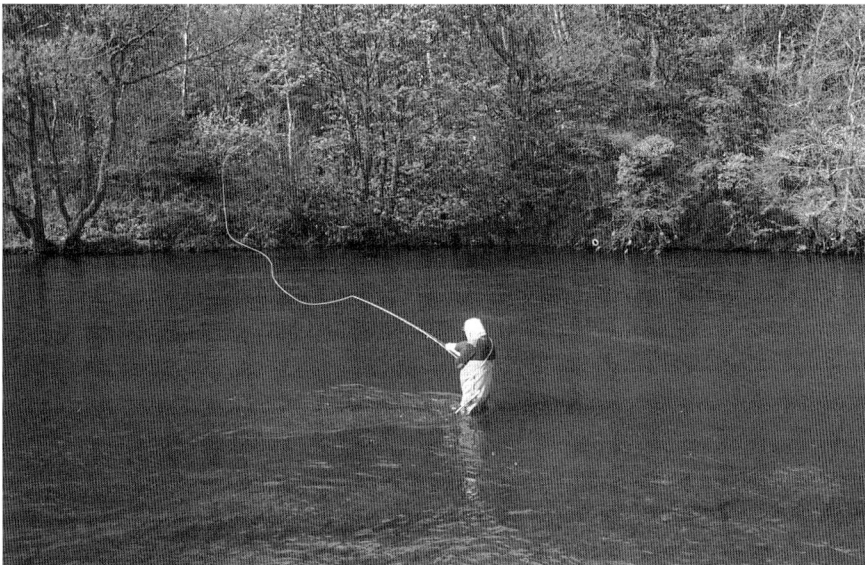

... and carrying them out across the water towards the far bank. A cast of extreme simplicity and perfect safety, which can be made in virtually any weather conditions.

Although the build-up of the figure-of-eight Spey cast is automatic, remember that the final roll cast is not. To make this cast perfectly demands perfect timing from both your forearms and wrists. This will not materialize by magic. You must practise …

Practise …

Practise …

The power stroke of a roll cast finishing off a single Spey cast. Notice the surface disturbance forty-five degrees upstream of the angler's right shoulder. Although in nearly every case this proves innocuous, there are certain low water conditions when this might affect salmon taking behaviour – or (more likely) that of an angler who is sharing the pool and fishing down behind. In such a situation it is only polite to change one's technique. From the right side of the river – casting to the left – this can be done with a roll cast off the right shoulder in the normal way. From the left side, a reverse roll cast can be made with equal effect.

## THE ROLL CAST IN FLY PRESENTATION

I have heard it said that the roll cast is used simply in putting the fly back whence it came – to straighten a line, or bring a sunk line to the surface – but this is far from the truth. Both on the river and in still water it can also be used in fly presentation: a valuable cast in its own right.

As a Spey cast can be described as a re-directed roll cast, so a roll cast can be defined as a Spey cast minus the preliminaries – up to a point. That point being a change of angle up to about thirty degrees, one way or the other depending on whether we make a roll cast or a reverse roll cast.

By raising our arms higher than recommended by the pundits, and by using our left wrist as a back-up to our right wrist, we can prevent the line from being driven hard down on the water ("cut down" they used to call it), thus eliminating disturbance. But in the Spey cast, prior to the roll cast which finishes it off, there is always the splash of the line as it pitches on the "seaward" side of the angler.

In low water conditions on some pools a case can be made for using an overhead cast (provided there is room behind the angler and that it can be done without false-casting over the lies); but if the angler is wading and well clear of the bank, the water can usually be covered successfully by omitting the preliminary placing of the fly upstream, and using a straight-forward roll or reverse roll cast. That is to say, a *roll cast* made from the *right side* of the river, a *reverse roll cast* from the *left side*.*

This, of course, is why the angler must be "well clear" of the bank as suggested above. There must be room for him to swing his rod on the inshore side. Alternatively, if he is fishing from the bank itself it must be totally unobstructed.

*Usually, when fishing water of this sort – say the tail of a shallow pool in summer – my inclination is to leave it alone until the sun has dipped behind the hill. Then, in the darkening, the fish wake up; the line on the water seems not to disturb them, and if the "run" is fresh, success is almost certain.

Reverse roll cast from left side of pool, made to avoid splash-down of Spey cast on angler's offside.

Line brought up towards "key" position on reverse side. (Plenty of room to swing the rod inshore.)

Hands high in the reverse "key" position. Rod tilted safely to the left. (Plenty of room.)

Final stroke made at angle downstream. Line shooting out clear of the water, taking slack line with it and heading for perfect touch-down. Totally free of all disturbance. A very valuable cast.

Even if like me you have left it very late in life to try to learn anything new, I nevertheless advise you to learn Speycasting.

Opportunities to fly-fish for salmon came my way in the early nineteen-fifties and for the next thirty years or so, because ignorance is bliss, I was content to fish with the overhead cast.

In recent years however, an awareness of the importance of Speycasting filtered into my brain. Now in the nineteen-nineties, I know that the opportunity to fish limited and expensive salmon fly-water without being able to use the various Speycasting techniques is extremely wasteful.

Recently I took four springers on fly when high water, strong winds, bank-scrub and trees, created conditions that reduced the amount of fishing available to the overhead caster to a fraction of what was available to me. Rarely have I experienced such deep satisfaction as I had when I applied one of the appropriate Speycasting methods.

In my professional capacity I meet many salmon fishermen, and I am conscious that for the last few years there has been an ever-widening interest in Speycasting. I sense that people who are unable to do it feel deprived. I forecast that the present Speycasting "buzz" will become global – and that ultimately the Japanese, who are the most prolific fly-casters in the world, will want to become masters of this supreme casting skill.

Fred Buller (Author, gunsmith, tackle-dealer and one of Britain's greatest all-round anglers).

*"Lazy man's" rollcasting*
Angler remains where he is as his line swings round to the dangle. Meanwhile, line is stripped in to keep fly on the move …

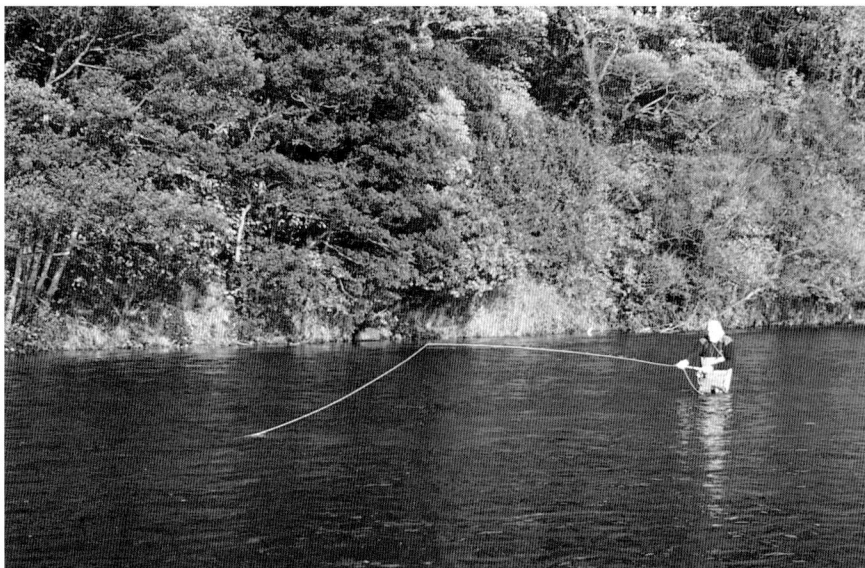

From the same spot the rod is raised in a reverse roll cast. Even now there is a chance of hooking a fish. (I have caught plenty in just such a situation; fish that have followed the fly and taken at the very moment of my making the next downward roll, with the rod at full stretch.)

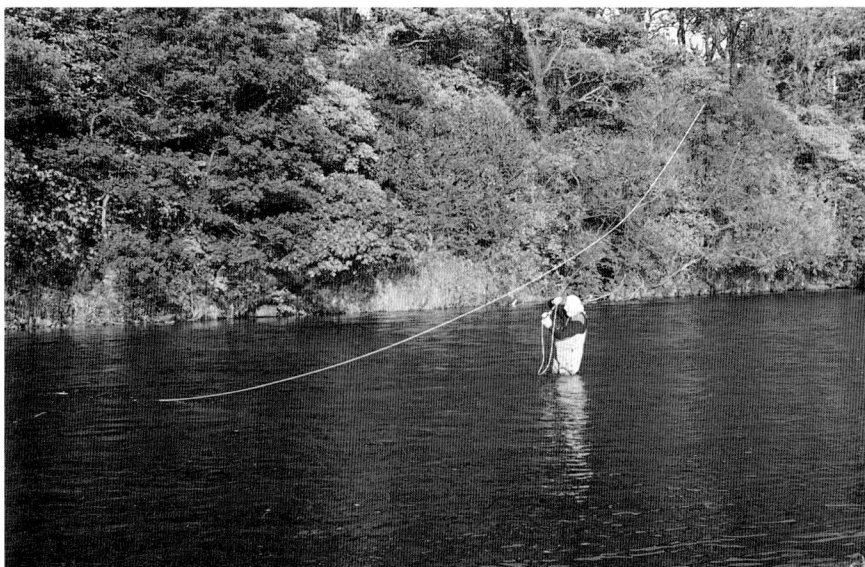

Reverse roll cast put out across the river. *Now* the angler makes his downstream move …

*Note*: As always, the angler's head and body have made no bobbing movements. The line is shooting out above the water and, for a roll cast, at a generous upstream angle. Why? Because the *rod* has done all the work.

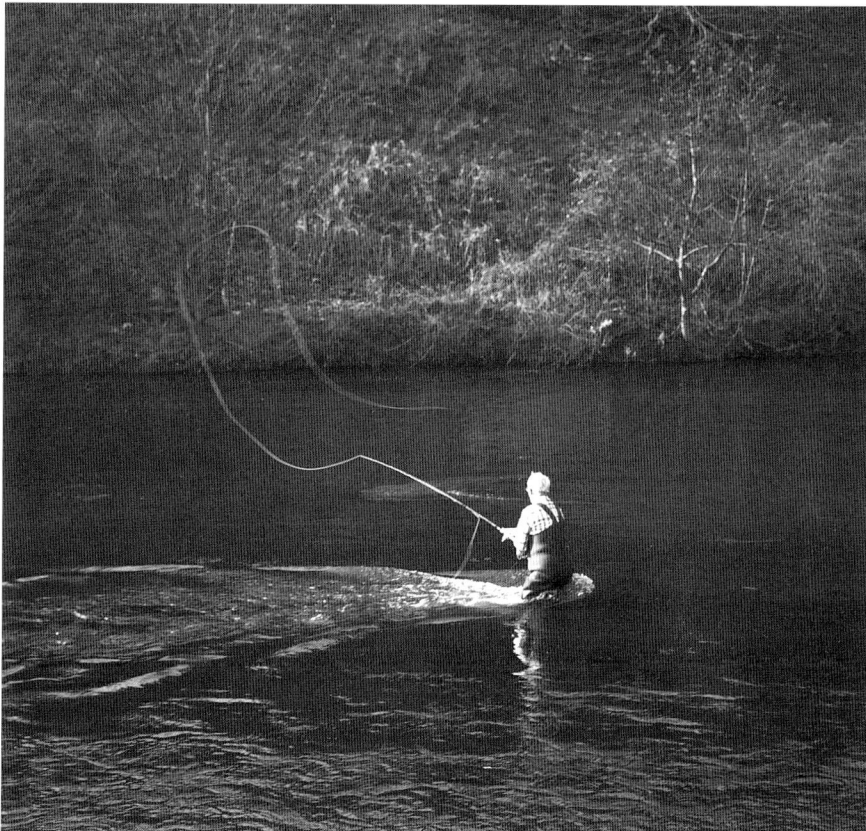

*"Mending" a line*
Bill Arnold's figure-of-eight Spey
cast goes curling out over a strong
current ...

As the rod comes down towards the
horizontal it picks up the line in
the air – before the belly has a
chance of hitting the water – and,
without pausing ...

... goes straight into what is virtually the start of another figure-of-eight. This time, however, it lasts only as long as it takes to turn the line over in a big upstream curve, or "mend", into which is shot all slack line gathered at the end of the last cast.

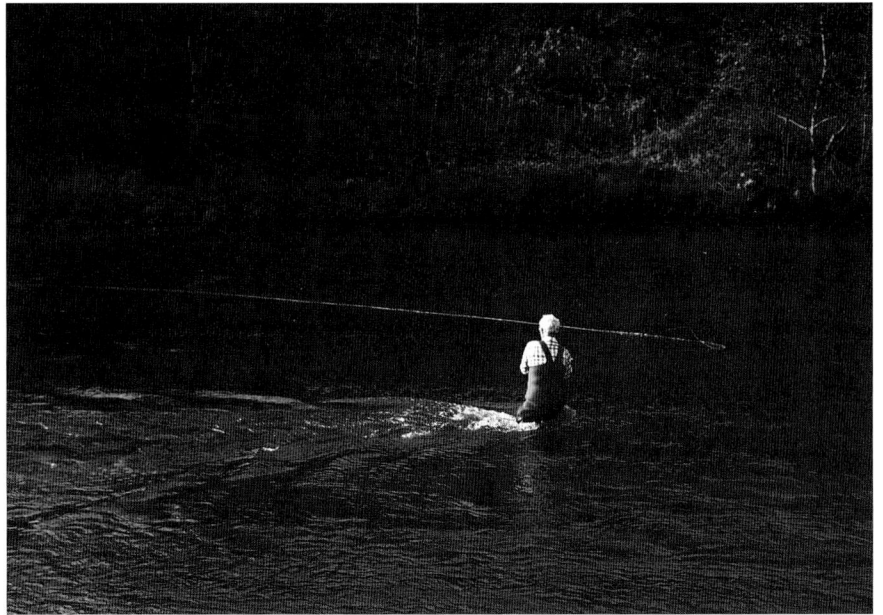

MENDING

Merely to cast across a strong current and leave the fly to swing round is pointless. As soon as the line touches down, the current starts to drag it round in a huge bow. So that, like the tail skater at the end of a "snake" twisting on an ice-rink, the fly comes whipping round at excessive speed, often skidding across the surface when on a floating line, and swimming far too close to the surface when on a sinker. In neither case is it likely to hook a salmon – although ultimately it may have covered every fish in the pool. We may have been casting thirty yards across the river, but nearly all of this distance has been wasted, for the fly was not working effectively until slowed to an acceptable speed – by which time it was hanging almost straight downstream from the rod. Not until the fly had reached that point would a salmon have been likely to take it.

Measured across the river, our effective range during each cast was nothing like thirty yards. It was, indeed, little over the length of our rod – if held out over the water at right-angles to the bank.

A distance of no more than six or eight yards!

Assuming we are throwing as long a line as we can, our effective casting range can be increased in two ways: by deep wading and by line-mending.

Mending is done with a circular movement of the rod, either when the line is still in the air, or almost immediately the cast has been completed, when the belly formed in the line by the current is switched over, so that the downstream curve becomes an upstream curve. This has the effect of slowing down the speed of the fly and causing it to move across the river in more life-like manner.

To maintain this semblance of life in a strong draw, several more upstream mends may be necessary as the fly swings round. But these can be made only with a floating line. When casting a quick-sinking line, we need to throw a big upstream curve just before the line touches down, shooting extra line as we do so. (See p.152.)

In a moderate current, mending is seldom necessary. The fly will fish round perfectly well if we leave it alone and let the current swing it over the lies.

When the current is sluggish we may need to go into reverse. That is, cast squarely across the river and mend *downstream* – perhaps shooting extra line in the mend. Here we purposely form a big downstream curve for the current to "bite" and help swing the fly across the stream.

Remember: mending should be done only on rippled water, *not* on flat, glassy surfaces where it may cause disturbance. And on no account across those smooth, shallowing pool tails which, in summer, are often potential taking places. When the river is low, these tails are better left unfished until dusk.

Speycasting in a blustery wind, it often pays to anchor the belly of the line for an instant before ...

There is an underhanded throw much in use on the Spey, which prevents the line from circling behind. Of course this is a great advantage among trees or other obstacles. It is generally practised upstream and *the line with its "swish" upon the water goes over all the fish before they see the fly, which* appears to me a great objection. These Spey fishers can throw this under-handed cast as far as an expert hand in the ordinary way. A peculiar rod is necessary, which must be very stiff. Indeed, a common salmon-rod would be apt to break in the hands of these fishers. The cast is easily learned, but must be seen to be thoroughly understood.

J. Colquhoun, *Rocks and Rivers* (1849)

An interesting passage, which helps to explain the reservation some writers have expressed about Speycasting.

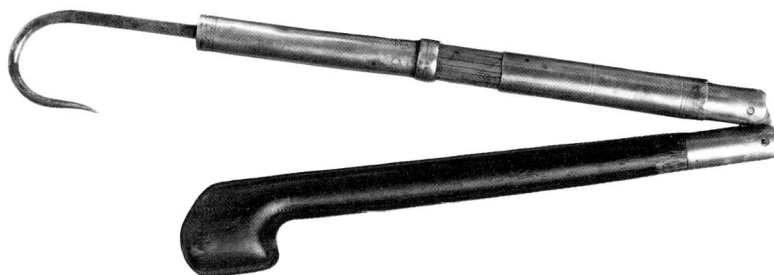

... switching it over and shooting all slack line in a big mend.
*Note*: In sunk line fishing there is only one chance of making a mend. If extra line is shot into this mend when we are casting across a strong current, we shall increase our chances of hooking a fish – because of the enlarged curve and its help in sinking the fly and reducing its speed.

# VIII   THE REVERSE SINGLE SPEY CAST

THIS CAST is made from the right bank of the river in an *upstream wind*. NEVER attempt it in a wind blowing downstream.

So long as you remember this piece of advice and keep plenty of tilt on the rod, you shouldn't have much trouble with it. The reverse single Spey cast is a direct mirror-image of the straightforward figure-of-eight single Spey cast, and just as easy to perform – once you have thoroughly mastered the reverse roll cast and bear in mind a few basic principles:

1   Swing from the hips to the left (without bending your body forward).

2   Keep your right arm straight during the placing of the fly at roughly forty-five degrees upstream.

3   Look at the spot on the surface where you want your fly to pitch (as recommended in single Speycasting).

4   Come up to the reverse roll cast "key" position keeping the rod *well tilted to the left*.

5   Put out a strong roll cast, using both wrists – particularly the left wrist with its inverted "screwdriver" action as already described.

> *Note:* The position in which you place the fly prior to the forward stroke will depend to a certain extent on the angle at which you intend to cast across the river. Often enough, our casting technique bears directly on the way we want our fly to fish. (See notes on traditional single Spey casting and sunk line Spey casting when moving downstream *after* a cast has been made, *not* between casts, etc.)

As in all Spey casting, until the forward stroke is made there are no straight lines. Nothing is angular or jerky about this cast. The rod never stops. It moves in a graceful, continuous reverse figure-of-eight curve throughout, starting by moving to the right, then swinging up and round to the left, and finally coming forward in a reverse-tilted power-stroke.

It may be of interest that I taught myself this cast some years ago when, because of injury, casting from my left shoulder with the left hand up the rod became very difficult and painful.

To my surprise, even before I had recovered, I found I could cast a longer, more powerful and accurate line by reverse casting than I could hitherto from the left shoulder.

Since then I have used it all the time when fishing from the right bank in a strong upstream wind, and teach it as an important part of my technique.

*Reverse single Spey cast*
We start with the line straight
downstream, then raise the rod in a
slight curve to the right so that ...

... it can swing up and round to the
left in a mirror-image figure-of-
eight Spey cast.

Swinging from the hips to the left and keeping the right arm straight, we bring the line curving just above the surface and guide the fly to its initial touchdown point about 45° above the left shoulder.

Meantime, the right hand continues its swing up above the head to its familiar reverse "key" position (left hand pushed well across to the right to ensure plenty of left-hand tilt on the rod). And while this is going on, a loop is forming in preparation for the reverse roll cast that will finish everything off.

Out it goes with a strong flick from both wrists, including (most important of all) the violent "screwdriver" upward twist of the left hand …

Straightening out *over* the water – to settle with a minimum of splash.

*Note*: The reverse single Spey is a very practical and powerful cast, but *never* to be attempted in a strong downstream wind.

Here we are *reverse single Spey casting* from the right bank of the river …

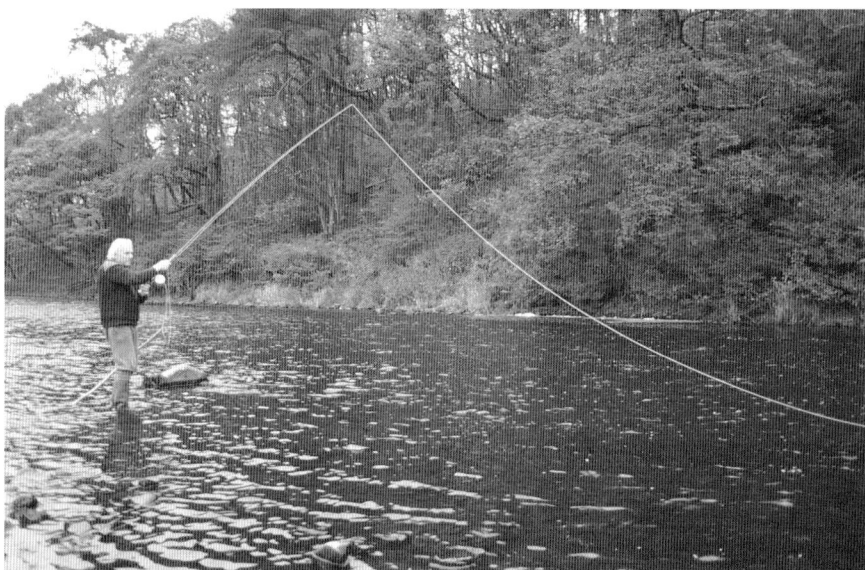

The rod movements should by now be familiar …

The mirror image figure-of-eight swing to the left …

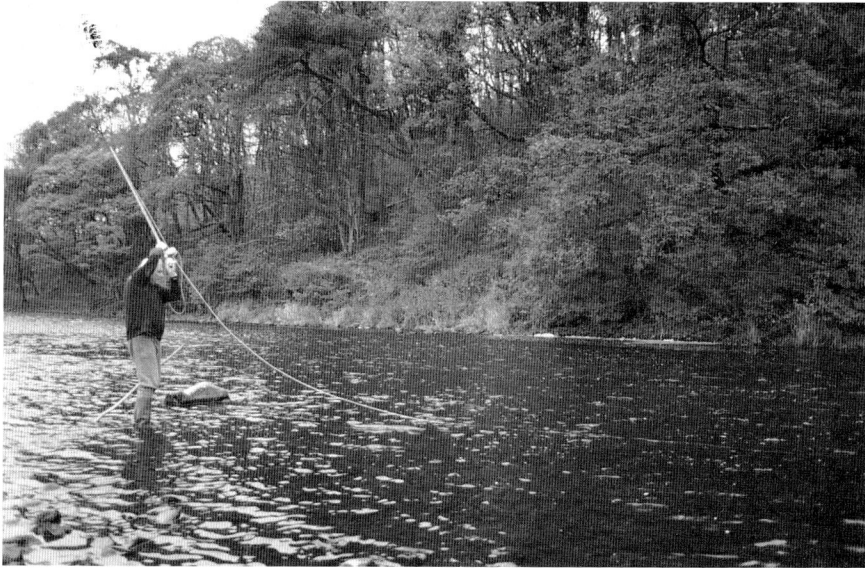

The rod sweeping up into the "Key" position …

A loop forming ready to be punched out – rod tilted to the left; line held well clear; no danger of the angler hooking himself in this picture.

And indeed out shoots the loop in a powerful ellipse. Showing once again (as in all our Speycasting examples) that this reverse single Spey has been nothing more than a re-directed roll cast.

Speycasting is like learning to ride a bicycle; the neophyte despairs of acquiring the art; but it comes, and in three or four days he is threading his way through crowded streets.

Or it does not come. I am acquainted with the owner of one of the most productive salmon waters in Scotland. I used greatly to marvel why he cared nothing for salmon-fishing, making mental comparison of his neglect of his beautiful stream with my own conduct were I in his place. I have since learnt that he once made a resolute attempt to learn the figure-of-eight switch at the hands of a past master. It was early in the season, when big flies are necessary, and it was blowing the usual gale. The lesson proceeded with the customary amount of injunction on the part of the craftsman and of expletive on the part of the novice, till at last, having attained, as he thought, to the exact degree of poise, the latter delivered a vigorous cast, and immediately was conscious of a violent blow and sharp pain in the lobe of the ear. The fly on a $3\frac{1}{2}$-inch hook, driven by the gale, had struck him on the back of his head, and the barb had buried itself in the gristle of his ear. That gentleman discontinued his lessons, has never resumed them, and lets his valuable angling rights.

Sir Herbert Maxwell; *Salmon & Sea Trout* (1898)

# IX   SUNK LINE SPEYCASTING

GENERALLY speaking, over the years fly casting with quick-sinking lines has not received much acclaim. When one considers the injuries that have been caused by heavy lures and big hooks, the wariness of many salmon anglers is understandable. Frightened, somewhat naturally, by the sound of a big tube fly with its attendant treble hook whistling past their ears when they are overhead-casting, and ignorant of how to deal with it when Speycasting, a lot of people are chary of fishing the big sunk fly and prefer (where it is permitted) to resort to spinning. But as I shall try to explain, once one's standard of rollcasting is good enough, sunk line fishing – with whatever density of line – is perfectly safe and straightforward. Correctly performed, it need present no danger, and can be fished with as much *sang froid* and confidence as a floating line.

If you study the rollcasting picture on p.150, you will notice a curious fact: at the completion of the power stroke in this roll cast, the rod has returned to rest in the horizontal position and is motionless, although the end of the line with leader and fly are still turning over. And unless the angler finds some useful task for it, the rod will remain unemployed until the cast has straightened out.

Becoming aware of this while practising, I thought it unnatural that during a cast the rod should come to a halt and have nothing to do.

A big lure tends to hang back and takes time to turn over. Wait for it to do so and the chances are that the belly of the line will have touched down and started to sink, so that it becomes difficult, sometimes impossible, to pick up into a Spey cast.

Working on how to avoid this, I made the happy discovery that on average the time taken for the fly and leader to turn over *after* the rod had come to a standstill in a roll cast, equalled the time taken in making the first part of a figure-of-eight Spey cast.

*So*, why not put the two together?

Surely there was *no need* for the rod to come to a stop. Without waiting for the roll cast to finish, after it had returned to the horizontal, it could go straight into the Spey cast without any pause whatever. And so it proved.

Thus was the figure-of-eight sunk line Spey cast born, the effect of which was far-reaching. It revolutionized my sunk line fly fishing overnight, and ever since it became part of my teaching programme, it has done the same for most of my pupils.

By now, one of the main reasons for my insistence on using both wrists and rollcasting *above* the water should have become abundantly clear. If a roll cast is made with sufficient power and accuracy, a sinking line (whatever its density) need never touch the surface until we have whisked it upstream in the Spey cast. Never again should our line "stick" to the water when we start a sunk line cast.

Once the technique is perfected, casting a sinking line becomes almost as easy as casting a floater.

But I must emphasize the importance of practice. Especially

the pick-up of the figure-of-eight *without stopping the rod*. This should all be done with a floating line until the timing is perfect. Master the various Spey casts, using this technique, with a floating line, and the sinker will present no problems.

When teaching this I have always made my pupils cast time after time until the pick-up becomes automatic with no hint of a hesitation. When anglers can achieve this with spot-on timing and are handed the sunk line rod, failure is very unusual. Almost without exception they will sail straight into sunk line casting with pleasure based on new-found confidence. Even though an hour before, it had all seemed like magic – and dangerous magic at that!

\*       \*       \*

Here is a ploy for the sea trout night fly fisherman fishing the Sunk Lure on sinking line in the deep part of a pool, perhaps the best holding lie for a big fish late on in the darkness.

Start three or four yards above the place where you would normally stand when covering that lie. Cast square across the pool, mending the line in the air, then immediately shuffle three or four yards downstream – allowing line and lure to drift with the current, sinking as they go. Fish the cast out from that spot, then as you draw the line in and prepare for the next cast, back up three or four yards. Then roll downstream to bring your lure to the surface and start again.

Provided an angler has that stretch of water to himself and is not being selfish or hindering anyone, this sunk line technique (which used to catch me numbers of big sea trout) will vastly improve his chances of success.

*The picture that says it all*
The power stroke at the climax of this downstream roll cast has brought the rod back to the horizontal position whence it started. But the fly – a big tube on the end of white quick-sinking line – is still in the process of turning over. Meanwhile, the rod is stationary. If we wish to go straight into a Spey cast, however, the rod should not be allowed to stop.
As it comes down to this position, without the slightest hesitation the rod should pick up the line in the start of a figure-of-eight Spey cast before the line has rolled out, and while it is still in the air above the water (see Ch. IX).

If you understand what is implicit in this picture your sunk line Speycasting problems are virtually over.

Using a white quick-sinking line, the angler has roll cast a big lure to the surface and then rolled it straight back downstream preparatory to making a Spey cast. The rod has completed its power stroke and come down to the horizontal position whence it started. *But* the lure, in the way of heavy flies, is hanging back and still in the act of turning over.

At this instant, without the slightest hesitation, the angler takes advantage of the delay by going straight on into a figure-of-eight Spey cast – swinging the rod round to the right and leading the line upstream *before it has had time to touch the water.*

By the time the rod is half-way round (at right-angles to the river) the fly will have turned over and plopped down – only to be plucked out again instantly and whisked away upstream.

After placing line and fly at forty-five degrees to his right shoulder the angler goes immediately into the final roll that completes the single Spey cast. Having only brushed the surface (but long enough for the "little hands" to take command) the newly-formed loop goes whizzing out across the pool. Again, *over* the water; so that, before the line touches down, the angler can throw his rod over into a big "mend", shooting into it, if he wishes to enlarge it, any slack line he happens to be holding.

After this, if the current is strong, *he will move downstream.*

Note: When fishing sunk fly in pools where you want to fish as deep as possible, *always* move downstream (if you are able to) for two or three yards immediately you have cast square across the current. This, plus a mend, allows the line and fly to sink while drifting for several yards before feeling the effect of the current. In this way your fly will work much deeper than it would have done if you had finished conventionally.

Remember this advice when boat fishing. Ask your boatman to let you back downstream immediately you have cast, *not* between casts. And while you are at it, cast square across the river – if not slightly upstream. Over the years, all this has caught me a lot of fish. It will do the same for you.

*Sunk line Spey cast.*
Using either one or two roll casts, depending on the depth of the line and weight of the fly, bring the line to the surface and roll it straight back downstream again – aiming high, so that the line will straighten *above the water*. Then, as the rod comes down to the horizontal – with a continuous, flowing movement, showing not the slightest hesitation – pick up the line into a figure-of-eight Spey cast.

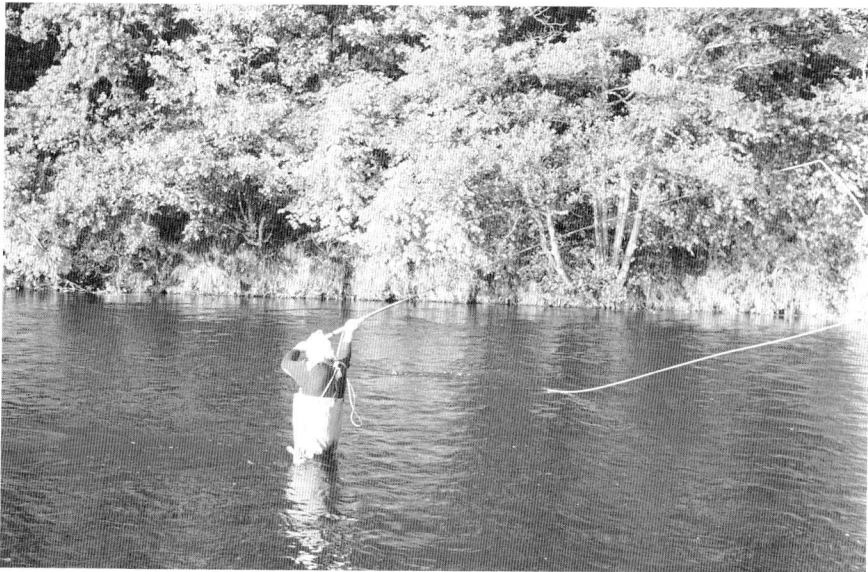

As you do this, swing round with the rod to the right, placing the fly in position about forty-five degrees upstream of the right shoulder. The line makes the briefest of touchdowns, merely brushing the surface, while the rod sweeps up through the "key" position and goes into the final roll cast …

… which punches the line out across the river.

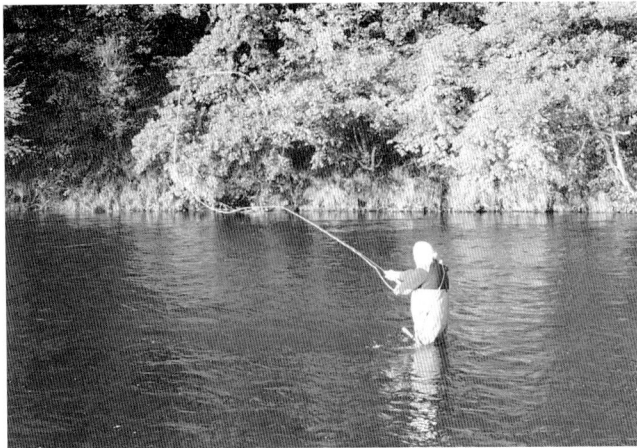

Again, this roll cast is aimed well above the surface …

… so that as it straightens out (a moment after this picture was taken) a mend can be thrown over upstream to the right.

To be successful almost all of our sunk line Spey casting takes place above the water …

Here the line is beginning to straighten out in the air …

Just prior to the final upstream mend.

Note: Once the figure-of-eight pick-up becomes automatic, and provided we cast only when there is an upstream wind blowing, the sunk line Spey cast loses all its danger. Once you have mastered it, never again will weather conditions persuade you to abandon the water or to resort to spinning – unless you wish to.

*Sunk line double Speycast.* (from the right bank)

We start by making a reverse roll cast (or two, if necessary) to bring line and fly to the surface from the dangle. Once you are confident the line will come free next cast, make a strong, determined roll back downstream making absolutely sure that the line rolls out *over* the water (according to the Gospel preached so far in this book). Then, without waiting for the fly to turn over and complete the roll, pull the rod sideways upstream to the left the moment the rod has reached the horizontal, while the line is still airborne and unrolling.

   The saving of time gained by this ploy (like the figure-of-eight pick-up in the sunk line single Spey cast, made in one continuous movement before the rod comes to a halt) is the *secret of success* with all sunk line Speycasting.

Here the initial reverse roll cast is made downstream to bring the line to the surface. (This roll cast has to be in reverse – from the *left* side of the body. If made from the right-hand side the rod would probably get snarled up in the bushes.)

The loop formed is punched into the air with enough power to send it shooting out above the water …

153

As we found in the single Spey cast, the rod arrives at the horizontal before the line has fully straightened and leader and fly have turned over …

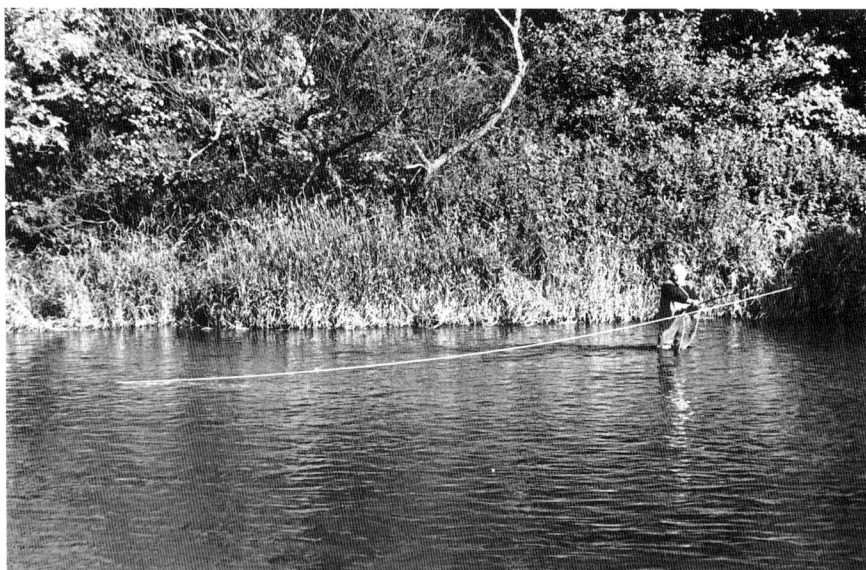

So, keeping the rod low (to prevent our line snagging the heavy fly as it turns over) we sweep it upstream to our left, swinging round with it from our hips and keeping the right arm straight.

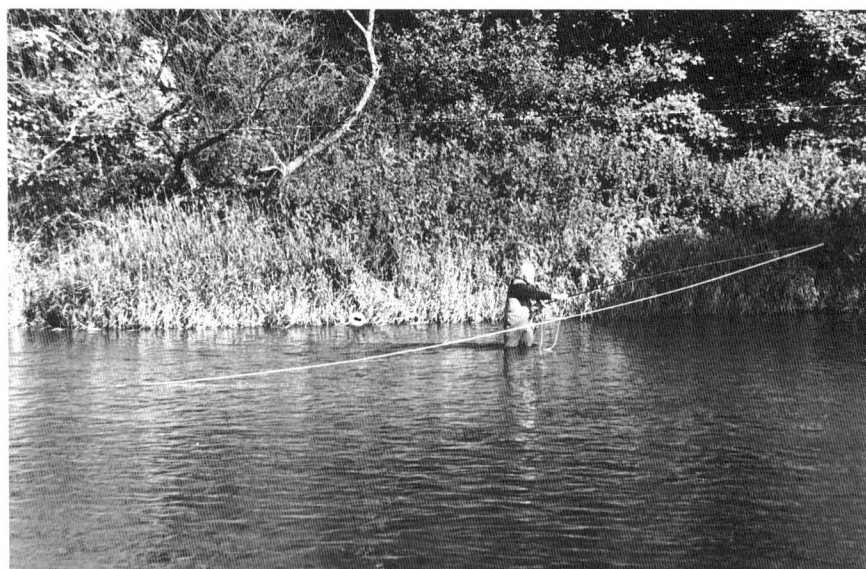

Now, with the line merely brushing the water, the rod is swept quickly back downstream and up to the right to form a big loop …

... which is swung through the "key" position of the roll cast ...

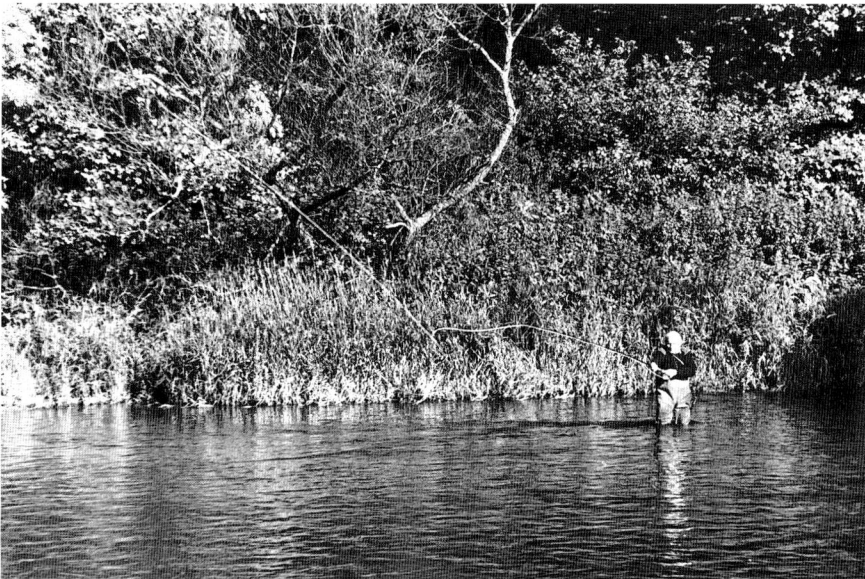

... and out across the river at whatever angle has been decided. Again, this power stroke *must* keep the line in the air so that an upstream mend can be made, if needed, to complete the cast – before the line touches down and "sticks" in the water.

Once more the dependence of Speycasting on accurate rollcasting becomes obvious.

*Note*: Sunk line casting must on no account be rushed. All the same there is no time to be wasted, or the line will "stick" in the water on its upstream journey. It demands the split-second timing that results from hard practising with the floating line.

# SPEYCASTING – A REMINDER

1 Position your feet at 45 degrees with your weight on the foot under the shoulder you are casting from.

2 Keep this foot slightly forward of the other foot and pointing in the direction you wish to cast.

3 Keep your thumbs on *top* of the rod butt.

4 To ensure forming a large enough loop, lift your reel to eye level in the "key" position.

5 Don't *thrash* the line from 2 o'clock. Simply accelerate the rod-tip to 11 o'clock, then check it suddenly with a strong flick.

6 Use *both* wrists – and roll the line out in the air. (Your bottom hand is *not* used as a pivot.)

7 Ensure that sufficient line is kissing the water as you make this forward stroke, otherwise the line will *crack*!

8 Stand upright and make the rod do the work. Don't bend your back, *push* the rod or roll your shoulder.

9 In single Speycasting, swing from the hips in advance of the rod and look at the point on the water upstream where you want the fly to land prior to the power stroke.

10 Avoid casting with the rod vertical. Keep the rod tilted so that the loop is well clear of you. When casting with strong to gale force winds blowing behind you, keep the rod tip moving forward from 2 o'clock to 11 o'clock faster than the wind speed – thus maintaining a perfect loop.

REMEMBER: Good Speycasting demands a perfect loop.
STAND UP STRAIGHT. KEEP YOUR SHOULDERS STILL. USE ONLY YOUR WRISTS AND DON'T PUSH.

When practising your casting bear in mind that to strive too hard for distance is a great mistake. Frustration, due often enough to fatigue, will tend to make you go on struggling for too long at a time, with the result that your shoulder and body movements start to creep in again. Your rod is no longer given the chance to do the work and you find yourself back where you started: the belly of the line hitting the water, with leader and fly falling in a heap.

Relax. Keep still. Concentrate on accuracy. You will be surprised to find how far you can cast when you are not *trying*.

Speycasting and its variations really can make the difference between success and failure. This was brought home to me quite dramatically when, with a party of friends, I was salmon fishing in Labrador. It was early July and touch-and-go whether the fish would arrive during our week. With two days of the trip remaining not a fish had been seen let alone caught. The camp was situated about five miles from the estuary mouth, and thinking that there might be some fish in the tidal pools we decided to take a trip downstream.

There, I walked to a pool immediately below some falls, sat for a while and watched. Suddenly, out of the corner of my eye I saw a fish break surface in the very tail of the pool.

At that place, however, the pool was in a deep gorge and the water studded with rocks. The spot where the salmon had moved seemed impossible to cover with fly. Overhead casting was out of the question. Spey or double Spey not much better because of the rock formation. Then, remembering the "Contrived Loop" cast I had been taught the month before, I sat on the bank and tried to work out how to do it. After a little while, like a jig-saw puzzle, it all dropped into place in my mind and I could see exactly what had to be done.

Perched on a rock I stripped line off the reel and let the current take it downstream. Then I roll cast a loop of line out between the rocks and followed it up with a powerful reverse roll cast. To my delight the fly shot out over the water and pitched exactly where I wanted it. As it swam across the pool tail there was a flash of silver and my line tightened . . .

Ten minutes later I sat fifty yards below the pool with a tide-lice covered $9\frac{1}{2}$ lb salmon, much to the envy of my companions. Sadly, we were unable to remain because of the tide and we had to cross a bay to get back up-river.

There was great celebration that night coupled with anticipation that the camp pools would be teeming with salmon the following morning.

But in this we were disappointed. After a fruitless hour up-river by the camp, I persuaded my guide to take me back downstream to the scene of my earlier triumph. Within an hour, from the same lie as before, I had two salmon on the bank, identical to the fish of the previous day and caught with an identical cast.

The rest of the party remained fishless. Unfortunately none of them could make the essential contrived loop cast, without which that lie was virtually impossible to cover. For me it had put three fish on the bank and, in enjoyment, had done much to justify the time and expense of crossing the Atlantic.

Anthony Desbruslais (Concert cellist, Barrister-at-law and all-round sportsman), from an article.

## X   THE CONTRIVED LOOP

THIS is a beautiful cast. So easy to learn; so simple to perform. With either double-handed or single-handed rod it makes possible what sometimes seems to be impossible, and enables us to cover fish that would enjoy immunity from any other form of fly casting.

The need for it arises when there is insufficient room between our line and the bank to lay enough loop on the water to avoid cracking off the fly. (See control of the loop in rollcasting by the "little hands" in Chapter II.)

To compensate for this we make space for ourselves in the form of a "contrived" loop of line, rolled out for eight or ten yards straight in front of us. Rather as a batsman at cricket makes room for himself to cut a ball that otherwise would pass too close to the bat, so we use the contrived loop to make room for the "little hands" to control what is now virtually a double Spey cast, or reverse double Spey cast, according to which bank we are casting from.

The conditions that conspire to bring this about are, usually, a stretch of difficult water that is too deep to wade and/or bank obstructions of one sort or another which preclude the making of any other form of fly cast. This situation may not often arise; but, when it does, the contrived loop cast can seem quite dramatic, making the difference between failure and success – as illustrated by the fascinating account from Anthony Desbruslais at the start of this chapter.

Essential requirements for making this cast are:

Gaps for your rod in bankside vegetation, and room in which to swing it.

A current strong enough to carry your fly downstream as you strip line off the reel.

The following two picture sequences brilliantly filmed from the right bank by Tony Mottram, and the third sequence comparably filmed by Ben Blackwell on stillwater as from the left bank, show it all in detailed clarity and explain the cast better than pages of words. Sufficient to say that success depends almost entirely on your skill as a rollcaster.

Take my advice. Grasp the principles of contrived loop casting. Practise it. Work unremittingly on the two roll casts which are indispensable – they will catch you fish on fly you may hitherto have thought yourself incapable of covering, except with bait.

During the years since I first conceived it, the contrived loop has caught me salmon in places I once passed by without a second glance. It has done the same for many of my friends.

\*　　\*　　\*

From my description of the cast one might think that it caused excessive disturbance; but, from my own experience, the special circumstances governing the use of contrived loop casting have seemed always to nullify any ill effects the splashdown of the loop might have. At any rate I can only report from my own as well as a number of other sources the high success rate this cast has enjoyed.

I ascribe this mainly to the fact that from start to finish in the over-grown bank conditions attending this cast, and aided by his background of vegetation, the angler is able to avoid the worst of all disturbances – the greatest cause of fear a fish can experience – the sight of the angler himself!

The following two photographic sequences, both shot from the right bank of the river, have been made in locations which, I hope, show the principles of the contrived loop cast as clearly as possible. (In practice, the banks would be covered with trees, undergrowth and other obstructions, making clarity of exposition very difficult.)

Here the rod has been held out across the river and line stripped off the reel to drift downstream to the required length.

Now the rod is brought upstream …

Not too high – so as to keep the line as far away from the bank as possible.

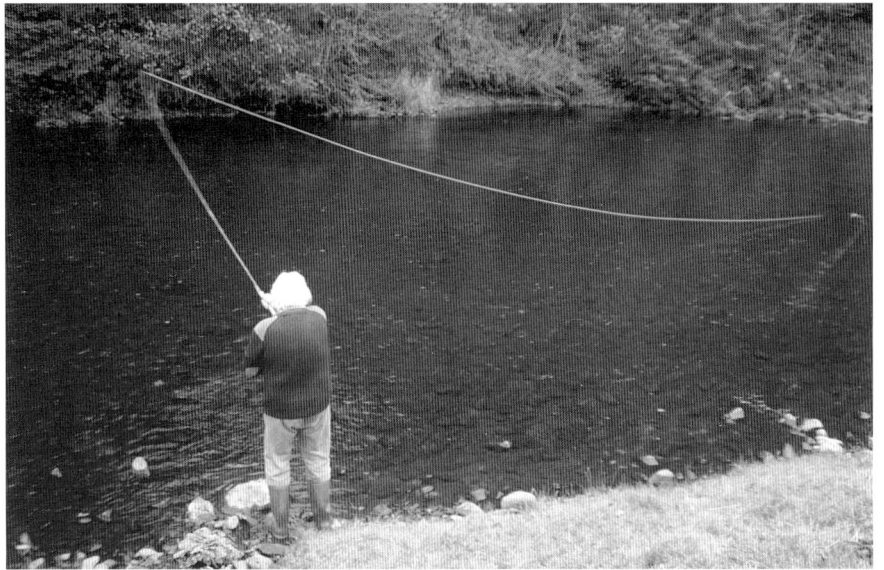

Now, as the rod comes to the limit of its upstream swing, it is raised ...

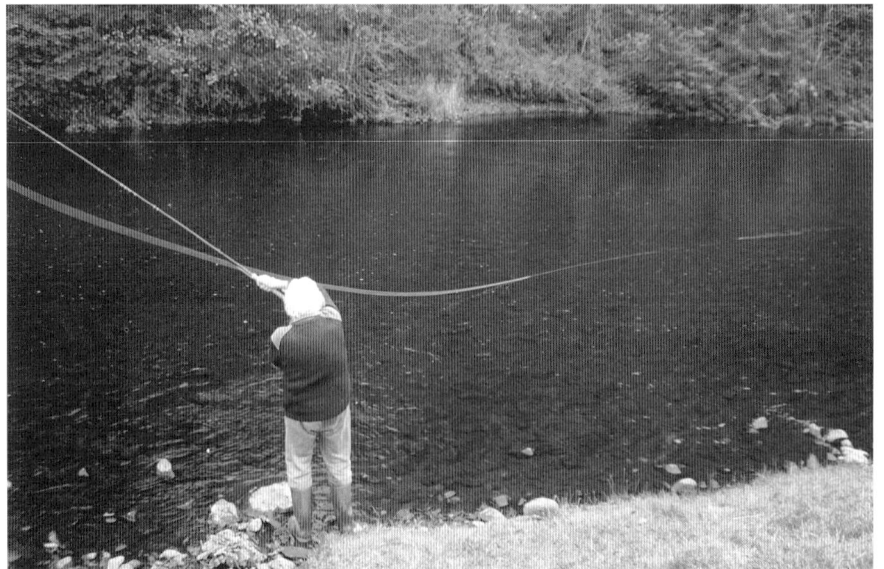

... to the reverse "key" position. A loop is formed on the angler's left-hand side ...

... and a reverse roll cast made with medium power – projecting a roll of line ...

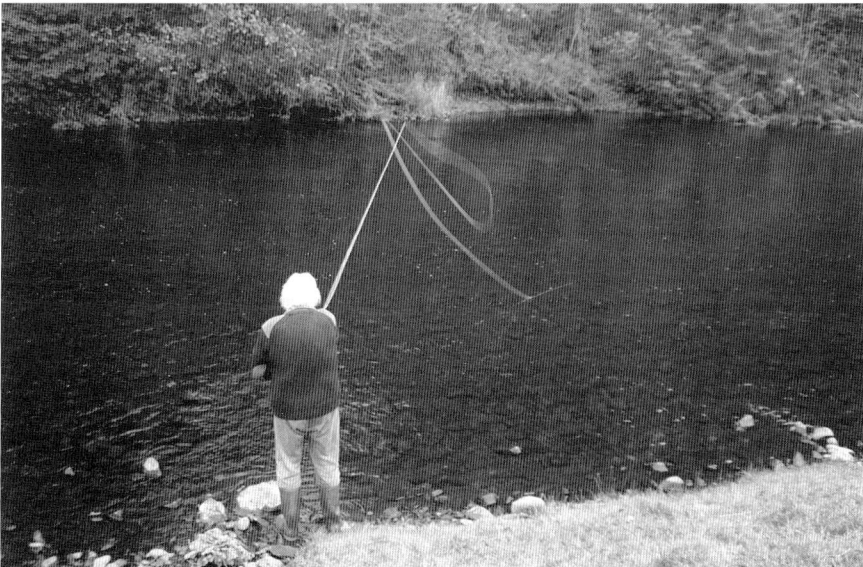

... straight out at right angles across the river ...

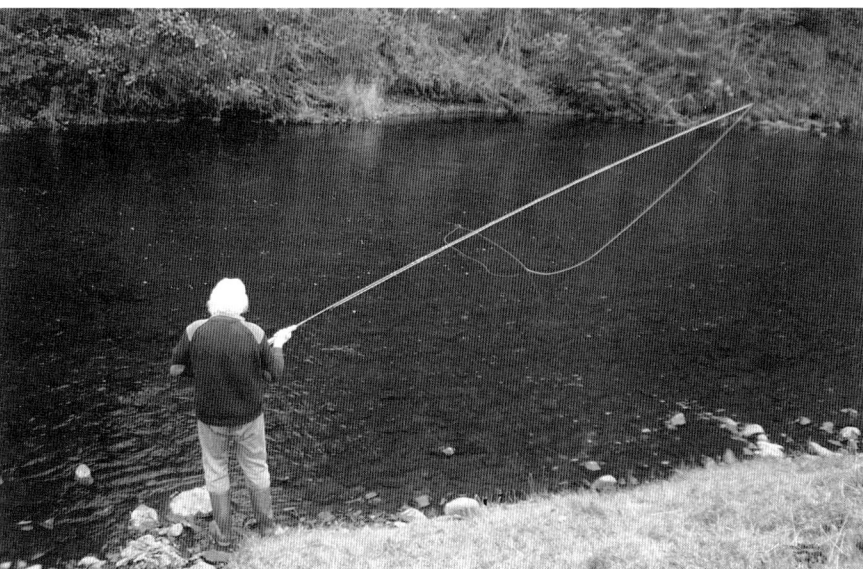

... resulting in a small loop on the surface. The fly having been left downstream, the rod is swung over to the angler's right-hand side, where it will stay.

Now, as the rod is raised, the loop on the surface unfolds ...

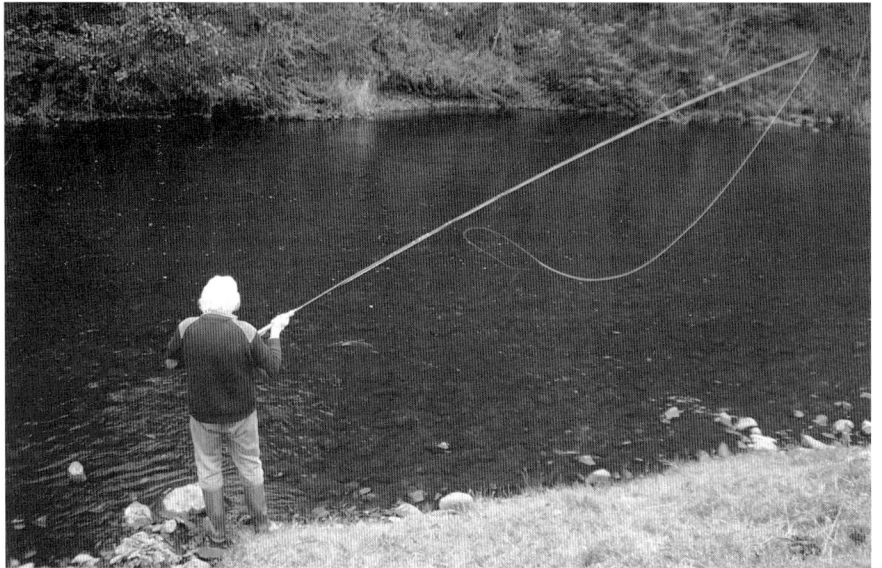

... and the rod moves on up ...

... towards the roll cast "key" position ...

... leaving on the surface sufficient line for the "little hands" to hold on to ...

... while the rod mounts higher still ...

... into the "key" position, and starts to move ...

... forward into the ...

... power stroke ...

... sending the contrived loop of line ...

... curling out right across the river.

Faced with the varying lengths of cork handles fitted to modern double-handed fly rods, anglers sometimes express doubt as to where the right hand should be holding it. The answer is simple. Bearing in mind that you should cast in an upright position, without bobbing to and fro or crouching, regard yourself as part of a right-angle triangle.

Standing erect, your body is the upright. Your rod is the horizontal base. Held straight, your right arm is the hypotenuse. So that to avoid leaning forward to grasp the end of an over-long handle, hold the cork grip at the place where your right hand meets it. For much of the time you are casting you will find that this is the most relaxed and comfortable position.

Here, the rod has been poked out over the water, line stripped off the reel and worked out through the rod rings, and the fly allowed to drift downstream. (It is now that the extra rings at the rod tip (see p.207) will be found so useful – by helping to avoid line looping inside the top ring as described in Chapter XIV.)

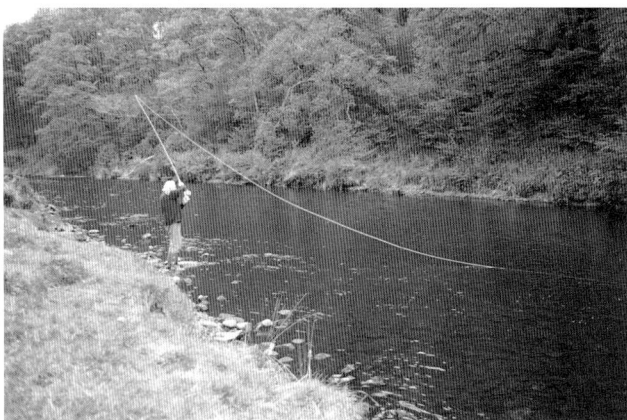

When enough line has been extended down-river, bring the rod upstream and swing it high into a medium-power reverse roll cast …

… that will put a contrived loop of line straight out at right-angles across the water.

It is essential that the fly remains downstream of the "contrived" loop. This can be achieved by cutting the rod point hard down and trapping the line as it comes upstream. This little ploy is difficult to describe, but easy to perform – and here the camera has caught the moment of contact to perfection. (It is just like a footballer trapping the ball.)

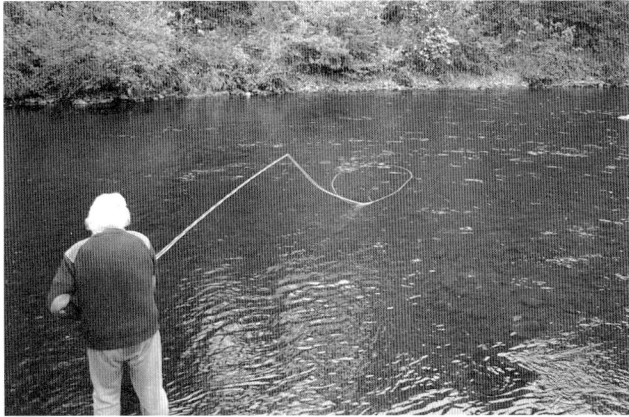

After this, everything is quite straightforward. Once the contrived loop has been placed at a suitable distance from the bank you can relax. There is no rush. The current will carry the loop away downstream. Let it go for a yard or two, while you prepare yourself for the final assault. It will help to line up the cast.

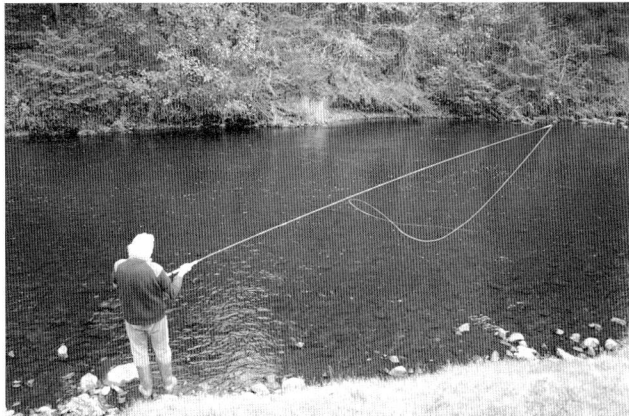

While this is happening, swing the rod over to your right-hand side in preparation for a powerful roll cast across the river. In slow-motion we can see the line straightening the loop ...

... as the rod is raised.

Because the line leading to the rod is always on top of the line leading downstream to the fly, there is no possibility of a hang-up.

169

Contriving a loop as we have, out in the river, away from the bank, has ensured that there will be plenty of room on the water from which to make the final roll cast.

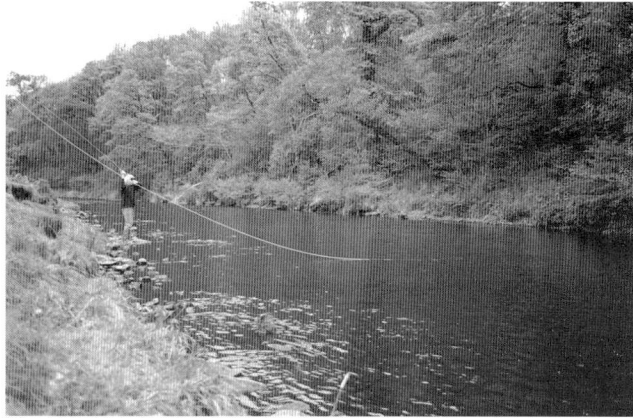

That is, a working length of loop gripped by the water tension which will control the strength of the power stroke and permit the line to curl over and extend without cracking.

And away it goes ...

... sailing out across the river.

I say then, and will maintain, that a salmon-fisher should be strong in the arms, or he will never be able to keep on thrashing for ten or twelve hours together with the rod eighteen or twenty feet long, with ever and anon a lusty salmon at the end of his line, pulling like a wild horse with the lasso about him. Now he is obliged to keep his arms aloft, that the line may clear the rocks; now he must rush into the river, then back out with nimble pastern, always keeping a proper and steady strain of line; and he must preserve his self-possession, "even in the very tempest and whirlwind of the sport," when a salmon rushes like a rocket. This is not moody work; it keeps a man alive and stirring.

William Scrope, *Days and Nights of Salmon Fishing*.

*Contrived loop as from left bank*
We start with the line stretched out close to the bank as it would be on the river if stripped off and allowed to drift downstream ...

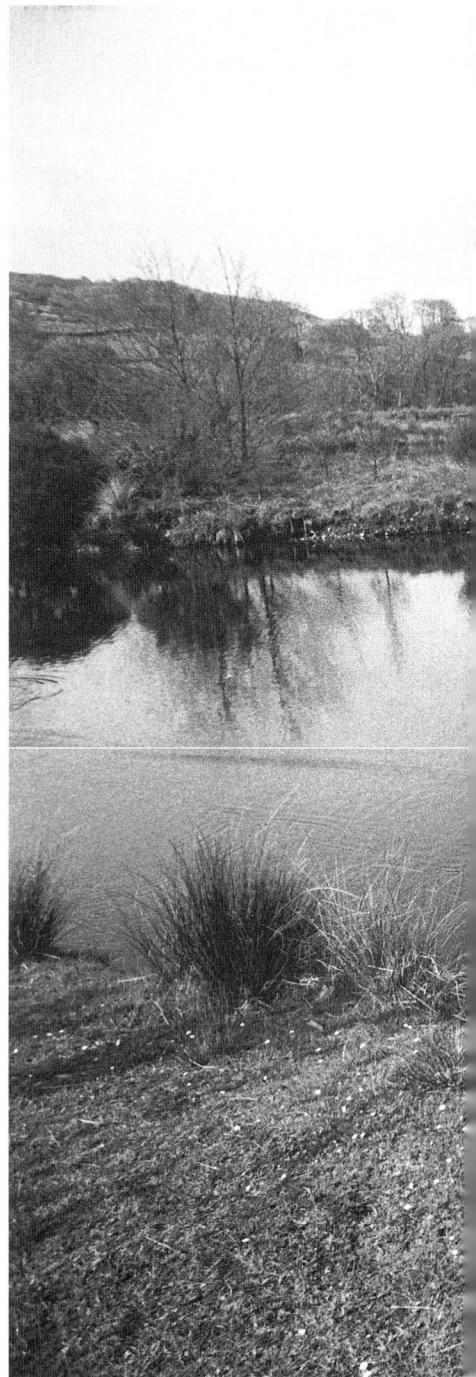

... the rod is swung to the right, with the line following in a steady glide ...

As the rod is raised towards the roll cast "key" position, the "contrived" loop begins to form ...

... the roll cast is made from the right hand side ...

sending out an elliptical loop of line low down towards the surface ...

... landing eight or ten yards out. The fly now is a short distance downstream to the left ...

... at this point on the river there would be no hurry. The current carrying the loop downstream is a help, since it makes the lining-up of the cast much easier.

There is plenty of room now to lay our reverse loop on the surface and complete the cast.

Notice how the tilted rod keeps the loop of line well clear of the angler's lefthand side.

Now we are up in the full reverse "key" position ...

To avoid getting hooked up, the final forward stroke must be made in reverse. The rod is tilted across to the left and raised into the reverse "key" postion.

... from which we can punch out
the loop, which in turn ...

I have often been told by "experts" that Speycasting tuition on stillwater is "out of the question" (I was once assured so by a former world casting champion) because "there is no draw on the line". But they are all wrong. They seem to forget that in practice we often have to roll cast back downstream in a belt of stillwater at the sides of fast-running rivers where our fly finishes up, often in a back-eddy, and the line is all scriggled.

If you learn to roll cast on stillwater, which is how I prefer to teach, you will be proficient *anywhere*.

H.F. – as an afterthought.

... picks up leader and fly and pitches them far out across the water under the loom of the distant bank.

Practise this cast every time you go to the river. You will soon discover how delightfully easy it is to perform. But you must be as skilful with one roll cast as the other – and a lot of training is needed in order to make the contrived loop with just the right amount of force, neither too much nor too little.

# XI   UNDER THE TREES

IT IS entirely due to the various forms of roll and Speycasting that we are able to fly-fish such difficult, but intriguing, stretches of water as that shown in the following pages. For want of a better title I have called it the Side Under the Trees – which is how my friends and I describe it on the beat we fish. It can be duplicated on many salmon pools in wooded river valleys. Nearly always such a heavily wooded bank is on the deep side of a pool and referred to as being the "wrong" side to fish it from – the opposite side usually having a gently shelving gravel or shingle bank from which nearly all the fishing is done.

There are, however, rewards in store for the fly fisher who can cover the water from the "wrong" side. Often enough it will produce a fish when sport is meagre and the opposite bank (the "easy" side) fails to draw an ace.

There are two possible reasons for this:

*First*: The fish have not been disturbed by the sight of an angler fishing on the open side of the pool and, perhaps, wading too deep.

*Secondly*: The direction of the sun. On an east/west flowing river such as the one depicted, during the main part of the day, the water under a wooded left bank will be in shadow; and, where possible, salmon will seek the shade in preference to bright sunlight. True, there are many pools in open country with no tree cover whatever, where salmon have to make do as best they can; but I have found that wherever they have the choice, salmon prefer to lie in the shadows.

There are, of course, other reasons why enthusiastic fly fishers often volunteer to fish difficult water. They relish the chance to test their Speycasting skills; to meet the challenge which is never deeply hidden in any field sport and is similar in many ways, I suppose, to the challenge so eagerly sought and accepted by the dedicated mountaineer.

The deep personal sense of achievement which exults in the defeat of heavy odds is perhaps part of the true sportsman's psyche. For such a person, the fish caught from some "impossible" lie represents so much more than the row of carcasses slain on easy water under the direction of a skilled gillie – or from a boat, placed "on the lies" by a local professional who has done all the work and in reality is responsible for catching all the fish.

My old friend and fishing mate, Bill Arnold, who always seems blissfully happy fishing Under the Trees, has kindly jotted down some thoughts about it:

> I derive great pleasure from fishing this pool from the deep side. The wading is tricky, being slippery and uneven and of variable depth. The current is strong in places, with a vicious back-eddy near the bank under the tree branches. But there are some good taking lies among the big rocks – if one can overcome the casting problems caused by the high bank and the trees, continue to put out a good line and then control the speed of the fly.
>
> Salmon fishing means a lot more than just killing fish. What

really matters to me, and has done for so many years of my life, is how I catch them, and where. To take a fish from this stretch gives me a huge feeling of satisfaction – more so than from any other pool on the beat, simply because it represents such a challenge.

I know it does to all of us who fish it. Besides, irrespective of results, we all get so much pleasure from our casting.

Casting a line underneath and around the ends of tree branches soon emphasizes the importance of practising one's roll casts with varying degrees of tilt on the rod.

Bill Arnold fishing down a long pool from the deep side in front of a steep, densely wooded bank. An overhead cast would throw no dice. Here one needs roll casts, Spey casts, reverse double Spey casts as well as the contrived loop, according to variation in the branches, gaps between the trees and the changing depth of water.

Almost as difficult a stretch of fly water as one could find.

I shall never forget the rueful countenance of one who, some years ago, rented a salmon-fishing in the south of Scotland, and engaged the friendly offices of a local expert to teach him the trick. One fine morning in April, on my way to a higher beat on the same river, I saw from the road this couple at work on a celebrated cast. I stopped the dogcart and went down to see if they had met with fish. The stranger was sitting on the bank with a most melancholy expression on his features, and beside him lay three lovely spring salmon.

"You have done pretty well!" I observed.

"Oh," said he, "*I* didn't catch 'em; it was Major S——," pointing to his instructor, who, up to his middle in the water, was doing his best to turn the trio into a quartette.

"I am showing Mr. A—— the water," cried Major S—— over his shoulder, with a twinkle in his eye. He had allowed his pupil to try his hand first, and, after he had utterly failed to get the fly into the desired quarter, had gone in himself with the result described.

Sir Herbert Maxwell: *Salmon & Sea Trout* (1898)

## XII CASTING OFF LEFT SHOULDER

WHEN ALL the casts can be made competently from the right shoulder, left shoulder casting should prove simple enough. The rod movements and casting principles have all been worked out. You have simply to make them from the other shoulder. It is only a matter of practice: doing exactly what we have been doing, only in mirror-image. The left hand is above, the right hand below, on the butt. The grips are the same – thumbs on top, and now the right thumb occupies the little groove. The feet are set at about forty-five degrees, only now the left foot is slightly forward and pointing in the direction of the cast. And now we are casting off the left leg.

From my own experience I found that what took longer to master than left-handed casting was the right-handed use of the wading-stick. I never wade without one, but skilful use of a weighted stick demands a lot of practice – if it is to become a part of one's body; a third leg. Properly used, a wading-stick is a great blessing. Used without understanding, it can be a curse. Practice, it has been said, makes perfect. Well, let nothing stop you practising.

To be able to cast off either shoulder is very handy. For me, essential, since I have occasional pupils who are left-handed and have to be taught on that side. But it is important that if we are going to make ourselves ambidexterous we should do it thoroughly and not shirk the *reverse* casting.

The inability to reverse cast nearly cost a companion his life a few years ago. We were sharing a long pool from the left bank below a high cliff and there was a very gusty "headstrong" wind. Waiting for him to get about halfway down the pool before going in myself, I sat on the bank and watched him fish. He was wading deep and putting out a competent Spey cast in the strong upstream wind. But suddenly the wind switched and he was caught by a vicious downstream blast. (In effect it was similar to the casting conditions described on p.100.)

Realising as his fly swung round to the dangle that he had no chance of making another single Spey cast, he switched hands and started to make a left-handed double Spey cast.

Halfway through the cast, another, even stronger gust, hit him. He staggered in the fast current and fumbled desperately for his wading-stick – which was now on the wrong side of his body! Despairingly he tried to change hands again and grab it, but too late. His feet slipped, and away he went into deep water.. Dropping his rod with a cry of terror, he threw up his arms and disappeared.

Well, I fished him out. No story in that. He was only a little chap and didn't struggle much. After all, I had learned about life-saving when a schoolboy, and had been putting it into practice ever since. Besides, I had seen it all happen before and the moment he stumbled I had started to run down the bank.

Afterwards, while our waders drained, we sat side by side on the fishing seat finishing a flask of Scotch from his tackle bag.

"Jesus!" he said. "I was lucky you were there. It all happened so quickly. I was panic-stricken. I didn't have time to think about it.   One moment I was fishing quite happily, the next … " He shook his head and shuddered. "My God! How easy it is to finish up face down at the tail of a pool. When I think of my wife and family …"

"I saw exactly what happened," I told him. "The wind switched downstream and caught you off-balance. But you were crazy to change hands in that current. Why didn't you just make a *reverse* double Spey cast?"

"Never heard of it," he replied.

"Well," I said. "You'd better hear about it now. I'll show you how to do it."

In the late afternoon sunshine, clad in wet underclothes and stockinged feet, I gave a brief demonstration of reverse double Speycasting. He watched, fascinated.

"Hell!" he said. "That's brilliant. You ought to teach that to people."

As near the vertical as the rod should come. Tilted at an angle of about 2 o'clock to the left. A perfect "key" position. *Note*: There is no "casting out of the belly" here.

When practising, get a friend to watch you from a distance and criticize . That is how the great golfers learn to polish their skills.

If our rollcasting is accurate there is not going to be much wrong with our Speycasting.

Over and over again the "Spey cast" is discussed as if it involved some secret lore not less august than that of the highest Masonry; but it is a natural and simple action which would have come to pass, independently, at the instance of almost any intelligent fisherman, although it had never been heard of in rumour or in literature. Is any good purpose accomplished by making a mystery of the craft ?

W. Earl Hodgson
*Salmon Fishing* (1906)

Notice the way the hands finish up in this sequence. There has been no pulling back with the right hand. It has done its full share of the work, in conjunction with the left (which is now the master hand). Notice also the balance of the body: feet well placed, with *left* foot pointing where the cast is to finish up; angler's weight taken on the *left* leg. Remember these points when casting off the left shoulder, copy faithfully the rod movements you have already learned, and with a little experience you will soon get the measure of left-handed casting.

# XIII REELS AND REEL BELTS

ABOUT reels I haven't much to say. A reel is simply a spool holding a reservoir of line, attached to the rod. Strictly speaking it doesn't *have* to be attached to the rod. In fact, often it is better if it isn't. One very handy way of carrying a reservoir of line is to fasten the reel to a "reel-belt" strapped around your waist. This has several advantages over the conventional method: it makes the rod much lighter and is thus a great blessing to anyone suffering from injured muscles; you will not risk losing all your tackle if you drop your rod, either when on the river or from a boat, and you will increase your casting distance when you need to. Forget the notion of rod and reel having to be in balance. A rod will Spey cast perfectly well with no reel attached. You are usually doubling the weight of a rod when you fit a reel to it. As for convenience, it is only a matter of a few seconds to shift the reel to or from the rod.

Try it. As the illustration shows, it is a very simple gadget to make: part of an old rod-butt fastened to a curved base, which fits round the tum, cut from a small plastic barrel. Several of my casting pupils suffering from aches and pains have used the model shown with much relief. Indeed, I could have sold it many times over.

My advice on buying a reel is to get the lightest you can find, compatible, of course, with sufficient strength and reliability of action, and a drum large enough to carry sufficient backing – say, up to 150 yards. You will seldom need as much as this, but when you do you need it badly.

The place of the reel-belt in angling history is not without interest. When I first conceived it I thought I had dreamed up something new. But of course I hadn't. As my astute and gimlet-eyed publisher pointed out, a reel-belt was in use a hundred-and-fifty years ago: William Scrope refers to it in his *Days and Nights of Salmon Fishing in the Tweed* (1843). The narrator (a novice salmon angler) has just caught a grilse of which he is enormously proud …

> Long did I gaze on him, not without self-applause. All too large he was for my basket; I therefore laid the darling at full length on the ground, under a birch tree, and covered over the precious deposit with some wet bracken, that it might not suffer from the sunbeam.
>
> I had not long completed this immortal achievement ere I saw a native approaching, armed with a prodigious fishing rod of simple construction guiltless of colour or varnish. He had a belt round his waist, to which was fastened a large wooden reel or pirn, and the line passed from it through the rings of his rod: a sort of Wat Tinlinn he was to look at …

The narrator's scorn soon changes to chagrin, however, when it turns out that despite the shrunken state of the river, this uncouth fellow's bizarre tackle has accounted for two large salmon. That his method of fishing with the pirn at his belt was not by any means exceptional is shown by the arrival of another angler who "had a rod and tackle of the selfsame fashion". Scrope also includes an illustration of the scene (p.196) by Charles Landseer.

Incidentally, while on the subject of Scrope's book, it is interesting to note that water pollution from sheep-dipping is no new discovery. Referring to the state of the river, Scrope's "native" remarks to the newcomer: "They hae bin at the sheep-washing up bye, and she is foul, ye ken."

This question of angling "re-discovery" is very interesting and offers a fascinating field of research. In preparation of our book: *Falkus and Buller's Freshwater Fishing* (revised edition 1988), Fred and I combed the literature in search of re-discoveries. We listed quite a large number of gadgets, tackles and angling methods thought to have been modern inventions, but which, on investigation, proved to be up to several centuries old.

Perhaps the most dramatic was the "discovery" by our old friends Fred J. Taylor and his brothers, during the 1950's, of deadbait ledgering with fresh herring for pike. At the time, it was hailed in the angling press as a great breakthrough. In fact, however, the method – even the use of a baiting needle – had been described in detail by the author of *A Treatyse of Fysshynge wyth an Angle*, reputedly Dame Juliana Berners. (The Treatyse was first printed in *The Boke of St. Albans* 1496, supposedly hand-copied from the original manuscript by monks c.1450 and probably originally written c.1425.) Hitherto, we simply hadn't happened to have studied the book. Although this is something of a digression, it is so interesting that I quote the (transcribed) passage in full:

> Take a codling hook, and take a roach or a fresh herring, and a wire with a hole in the end, and put it in at the mouth and out at the tail, down by the ridge of the fresh herring, and then put the hook in after, and draw the hook into the cheek of the fresh herring; then put a plumb of lead upon your line a yard long from your hook, and a

float midway between, and cast it in a pit where the pike useth, and this is the best and most surest craft of taking the pike.

For centuries after that, however, the method fell into desuetude and stationary deadbaits were little used until, in post-war years, Fred Taylor developed improved rigs for this technique. From his writings a new school of pike fishing grew up.

Now, if Fred Buller and I ever prepare another edition of our work, the Falkus Reel-Belt can be added to the list of re-discoveries. Mind you, I am quite prepared for some clever dick to write and tell me that this book is all "old hat" and that my Speycasting technique was being practised centuries ago by North American Indians.

*Afterthought*

Further to buying a reel, don't let the tackle dealer seduce you into acquiring a spare spool. It is a curse; a time waster; a totally false economy. The saving of money is tiny compared with the advantage of having a complete reel and line ready for instant use.

A reel plus spare spool means that only one rod at a time can be set up. Whenever convenient, the sensible salmon fisherman will have two rods ready, with different lines, so that he can make an immediate change of tactics without the tedium of having to break down his tackle – a task he will not relish with frozen fingers on a chilly day. His failure to do so, however, will at times result in missed opportunities of hooking fish.

(It has long been my contention – often backed up with money when I was younger – that successful salmon fly fishing depends on much more than mere luck!)

Harry Otter (*kneeling*) confronts
local angler (with reel belt), from
*Days and Nights of Salmon
Fishing in the Tweed* by William
Scrope (1843).

Casting with the Reel Belt – left-
handed, to show the open side.
Notice, when casting off the left
shoulder the left foot is slightly in
advance; the weight is taken on the
left leg.

The Reel Holder Mk I has two body straps of its own. These are dispensed with in the Mk II model, which slips on one end of a Vulcan stretch belt – a great aid for elderly anglers at any time of the season, but especially during early spring and late autumn.

The Falkus Reel Belt Mk1

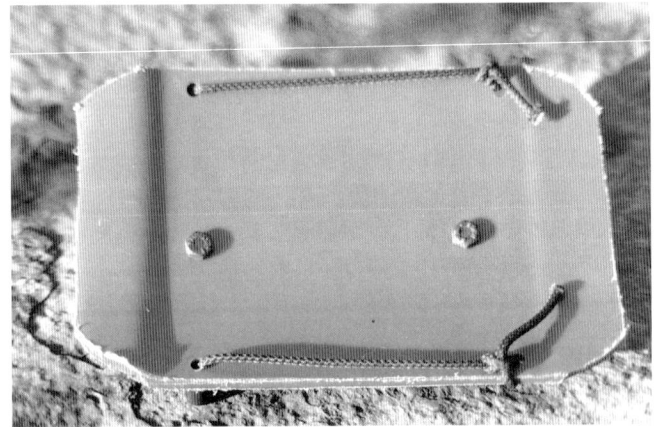

The Reel Holder Mk II. Bill Arnold knocked it up in our fishing hut inside half-an-hour.

In addition to providing warmth and comfort in icy winds or when we are wading deep in cold water, a Vulcan elasticated support belt for the back is a useful carrier for the Mk II Reel Holder.

Before you use a Reel Belt for fishing, try playing a "salmon" with it on land. Persuade an agile friend to hold the end of the line and run about simulating the antics of a hooked fish. You will soon discover the most convenient place for the rod butt; how to keep a tight line, and what it all feels like. A little practice is all that is necessary. You will have no trouble with it on the river.

Thoroughly practical though it is the design is open to improvement, and doubtless those of you who enjoy fiddling about will have a go at it. Anyway it is fun to play with and may help to keep some of my readers amused.

The two inside cord loops of the new model enable it to be slipped easily on the end of the body belt.

Casting with the Reel Belt Mk II. Picked off in separate shots from a number of casts to form a sequence, it shows how easily a long rod can be handled with no reel attached. A single-handed rod works just as fluently.

Note the complete absence of body and shoulder movement. There is no strain. It is all so comfortable and relaxed.

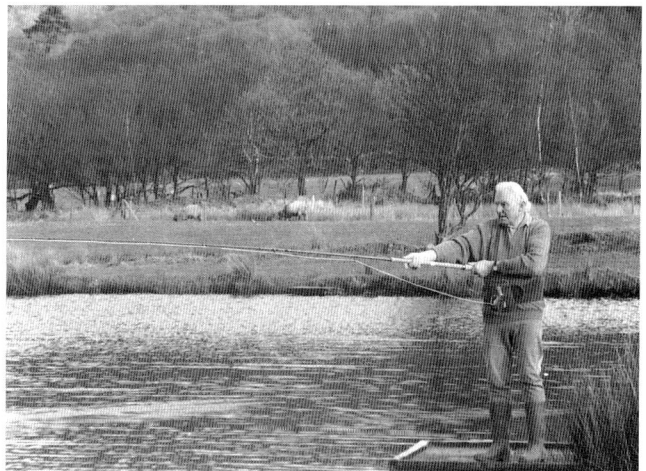

Note also, that many use to fish for a Salmon, with a ring of wyre on the top of their Rod, through which the line may run to as great a length as is needful when he is hook'd. And to that end, some use a wheele about the middle of their rod, or nearer their hand, which are to be observed better by seeing one of them than by a large demonstration of words.

Izaak Walton, *The Compleat Angler* (2nd ed. 1655)

The majority of salmon fishers probably begin their fly-fishing careers as trout anglers, and it is to those people that I wish to stress some of the differences between the two arts ... So many men take up salmon fishing late in life, and it is difficult to change the habits of many years. No two kinds of fly-fishing could well be more different ... a trout will discover the fly to be an imitation and reject it in the twinkling of an eye. Not so the salmon; he is probably not thinking of food at all, and just takes the fly from curiosity or playfulness. That being so, he usually holds it in his mouth for some little time before letting go, and I have seen fish chew at the fly for several seconds before blowing it out. It therefore follows that quick striking is taboo where salmon are concerned, and that the trout fisher, if he is to succeed, must discipline himself. That is one of the hardest things to do.

"Jock Scott", *The Complete Fly-Fisher* (1963)

## XIV TWO-WAY FISHING

ESSENTIAL to the wildlife films I used to make, a good deal of my working life was spent out of doors observing the behaviour of animals. All those hours were exciting and instructive, but none more so than the time I spent on river banks observing salmon. After a while it began to dawn on me that the fish I was watching was a different creature from the one so often encountered in print; that far from being fact, a lot of what I had hitherto taken for granted was fallacy.

Sometimes, indeed, the truth about salmon behaviour proved the very reverse of what had been claimed. Nowhere was this more evident than in the assertion of an eminent salmon fishing authority not long ago. Warning his readers against overfishing of lies and stressing the need to "rest" the fish from time to time, he wrote:

> Salmon get tired of seeing the same lure and when the novelty has worn off they are not likely to take.

He was not alone in thinking this. Regarded as an integral part of holy writ and handed on from writer to writer, it is a belief that can be heard voiced without contradiction on any salmon river: a sacred precept so obvious as to be accepted without demur.

It is, however, utter nonsense. As I have so often proved, salmon can frequently be caught by casting the same lure time after time in the same place.

For many years, in addition to having my own stretch of fishing, I had the good fortune to live within easy reach of several clearwater rivers in each of which fish could be observed and (as described in my book *Salmon Fishing*) I took full advantage of this. When conditions were favourable I watched the reactions of salmon to every type of lure that I could think of.

This observation of salmon-taking behaviour was a revelation. It led me to re-think much of what I had hitherto accepted as Gospel, for I soon realised that many anglers had written about what they *thought* salmon did, not what they had *seen* them do.

Their exhortations to "rest the water" – treating the salmon as they might a trout – was a case in point. Experiments with fish in view soon convinced me that if I really wanted to catch a salmon, the last thing to do was to "rest the lie" and leave the fish alone; that no matter how often a fish was covered, *provided he was not frightened* he might still take. And indeed, often enough he *did* take.

Now I am not suggesting that the best way of fishing for salmon is to stand in one spot and put cast after cast over the same lie. Too much of this would be dull and often unprofitable; it would, if someone else wanted to fish that water, be inexcusable. Nevertheless, the *potential* of this approach is worth some thought because, as my observations have shown, provided it is covered properly and the fish is not scared out of it, *a salmon lie cannot be overfished*, and I can assure anyone who understands what is implicit in this advice and knows when and how to make use of it that, in addition to approaching the sport of salmon fishing with fresh interest and confidence, he will undoubtedly increase his chances.

For example, belief in my axiom together with an understanding of floating-line technique and the use of perfectly balanced modern fly tackle, leads logically to the fascinating challenge of "Two-Way" fishing – a method I have devised for presenting a salmon fly wherein the fly can be worked both ways either across a current or in a loch without its being taken from the water.

A difficult, rather droll but very handy trick to have up one's sleeve, Two-Way fishing has caught me salmon I would not otherwise have hooked.

The principle of this technique is based on what I believe to be two important salmon fishing facts:

*First*: that if covered without causing disturbance a salmon lie cannot be overfished.

*Secondly*: that a fly fished fruitlessly across a salmon in one direction may sometimes be taken when fished in reverse – i.e., from the opposite side.

Often enough, except in the case of very distant lies or too strong a current, Two-Way fishing enables this to be done.

Two-Way fishing is made possible by the use of perfectly balanced tackle, expert roll-casting and the grip of the water's surface-tension on the line. Thus, when a big upstream loop of line is thrown so that the fly hangs so to speak from the far side of a "wheel", the line when drawn in will move around this wheel and bring the fly upstream against the current, or swing it back across the river. (While this is happening it is, of course, necessary to continue throwing loops of line upstream to compensate for the wheel's downstream drift.)

Two-Way fly control has proved effective in hooking salmon that had shown an interest; that had, perhaps, visited the fly but refused it. (As described in my book, this is the "Hamlet" fish; the salmon that cannot make up his mind!)

The diagram shows a salmon in a known taking-lie above a weir. To cover the fish in a conventional manner the angler (A) casts to B, mending his line if necessary (C) to control its speed as it swings round past the fish to D. At this point (the salmon having refused), a big loop of extra line is worked quickly out through the rod rings and roll cast upstream and across to E, a position well beyond the fish.

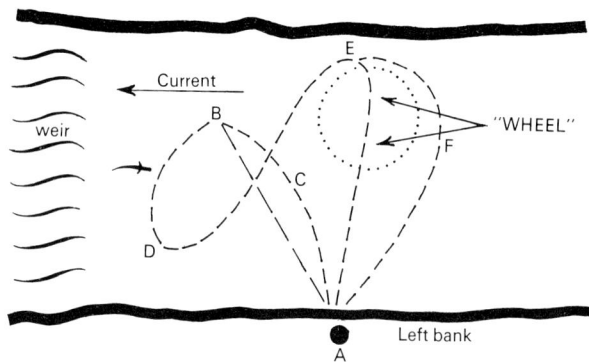

Two-way fishing or "fishing the wheel", as some of my friends call it.

N.B. This extra line, which was drawn off the reel *before* the angler cast to B and has been kept in reserve until now, must be cast *without jerking the fly at D*.

By skilful mending, speedy line retrieve and maintenance of the "wheel" by repeatedly working-out retrieved line and roll casting it upstream to F, the angler can make the fly swing back across the lie or hang stationary for a short time. With adroit line control he can even bring it round the wheel upstream against the current *away from the fish* – a ploy that sometimes *induces* a take.

This fly movement, backwards and forwards and upstream, can be kept going for a considerable time – provided there is not too strong a current or downstream wind. Far from being "put down", a salmon will sometimes take the fly after many minutes of such "goading".

Of all fly fishing methods, I have found Two-Way control the most fascinating. Since from start to finish the action is non-stop, it demands intense concentration and, like all juggling acts, you need to work at it, but once you acquire the knack of keeping the fly upstream of the fish it is utterly absorbing.

Try it. You will, at least, find it highly diverting. At best, rewarding. But take my advice – go and practise your two roll casts first.

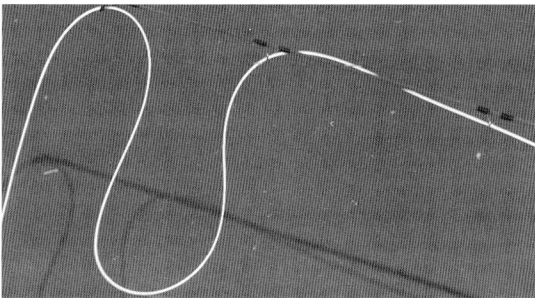

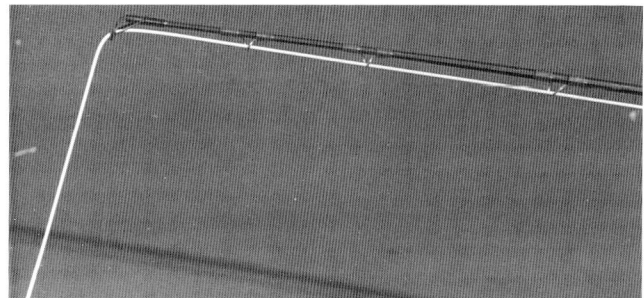

To be able to draw stripped line quickly through the top rod ring by sweeping the rod from side to side, keeping the point low so that maximum line is gripped by the surface tension of the water, prior to a roll cast, is essential to successful two-way fishing. It is also a useful method of lengthening line when we start fishing – eliminating any need to false cast.

If this is done too violently, a rogue loop will often appear inside the top ring. This is extremely irksome and disrupts the smooth continuity of the forthcoming roll cast, since the only way of getting rid of this loop is to pull the line back through the rings.

To prevent the loop forming, whip on a couple of extra rings near the rod tip. I have found this little dodge very successful. Today, all rods bearing my name are (or should be) equipped with these rings.

(*Note*: Ask the tackle dealer if he knows why.)

The story so far. Before this picture was taken the angler, wading down the right bank, has cast across the river and fished the fly conventionally round to his own bank. He has then made a big "wheel" around which he has allowed the fly to swing back. Then, having re-formed the "wheel", he is now fishing the fly round again towards his own bank.

His next manoeuvre (having gathered sufficient slack line and worked it quickly out through the rod tip) will be to make a fresh roll cast straight across the river (without moving the fly), mend it and fish the fly round the resultant "wheel" from where it is now towards the far bank of the river.

To fish the pool down or back it up in this way it is necessary only to shuffle slowly upstream or downstream in sympathy with the casts being made.

Much of one's success depends on the direction of the wind and strength of current. But it is a fascinating salmon fishing technique, and well worth the effort of trying to master it.

Most of my sea trout and salmon fishing is on small spate rivers, often tree-lined and overgrown. I have been aware over the years of missing opportunities to fish down awkward pools and runs too enclosed for an overhead cast, hence my long overdue visit for help and tuition. Amazing! It really is now a pleasure to use my single-handed rods with this newfound ability to roll and Spey cast, most certainly producing several fish from places previously beyond my casting skill. One of which was a 6 lb 9 oz sea trout, my best ever, following a reverse roll cast to a difficult lie at night. Just as important: what a pleasant and relaxing way to fish.

Ken Huggett (former Manx Grand Prix winner) from a letter.

*Two-way fishing on an Irish salmon lough*
The pictures show Dr Malcolm Greenhalgh the well-known freshwater biologist, author and fly-tyer, fishing the fly-only section of Lough Melvin – throwing out a loop, mending, re-throwing some more line to form a big "wheel", then trickling the flies along the edge of a wave, or working them in an arc *away* from the boat. A totally absorbing method of fly fishing, but one that demands a skilful and understanding boatman.

# XV  SINGLE-HANDED SPEYCASTING

ALL THE methods described in this book are just as easily mastered with one hand as with two. Except for dry-fly fishing, I never use anything else. Indeed I am hard put to remember the last time a wet fly disappeared behind me. As for waggling my head from side to side and working both arms like a semaphore, double-hauling yards of backing, I have never found the need for it. The Spey system offers all the casting distance necessary without flashing the line to and fro over the lies, in addition to ensuring safe casting in extreme weather conditions.

As with the double-handed rod, single-handed roll and Speycasting has huge advantages over back-casting, especially on bushy, overgrown banks, whether on trout streams or salmon rivers. Moreover the advantages when we are boat fishing are considerable.

I am reminded of professional boatmen years ago. There was no hope of work from the oars, no cross-wind fishing. It was a matter of drifting straight downwind (the most inefficient of all boat fishing methods) or nothing. This was not due to idleness on the part of the boatman, but because the poor bugger had been hooked too often. Head withdrawn, tortoiselike, beneath the protective oilskin hat favoured by most boatmen of those days, huge collar erected in the form of a carapace, he lurked underneath with shoulders hunched from one end of a drift to the other. The only evidence of life being a muttered imprecation when yet another wildly-executed overhead cast, caught by the wind, brought a team of flies clattering like buckshot across the oilskin hat.

But what a change in even the most fearful gillie a difference in casting technique could bring about.

At the rare sight of a polished roll cast, a wild gleam of hope would suddenly shine in the eyes. From beneath the carapace a head would start to emerge, cautiously at first, but gaining confidence. A minute or two later, as the roll and double Spey casing continued, in appreciation of its new-found safety, the neck would poke out into the sunshine like a tortoise at full stretch.

In no time at all, your boatman would be chattering merrily away and, having taken to the oars, putting you in all the best fishing spots. Yet another example (if it be needed) of how Speycasting can increase your catch.

\*     \*     \*

Two-way fishing, as described in the previous chapter, can be great fun from a boat; a pleasant diversion from more conventional methods. A light two-handed rod is useful, of course, but most of my own sport when loch fishing has been with a 10–11 ft single-hander.

A salmon as often as not will hook itself. Trout and sea trout are different. With them the big swathe of line leads to a failure to set the hook. But no matter. I have found the method a fascinating way of exploring the water – sending the fly (or flies) off on a tour of reconnaissance. When a fish rises, you have the lie marked down. The boat – which is being worked slowly across wind – can be checked and held in position, while the fly is retrieved and rolled out on a more practical mission.

It is delightful how often the ploy works. But so much depends on a highly experienced oarsman who is in sympathy with the method.

I know of few better day's sport on stillwater than one spent with a congenial companion who is well-versed in the skills of two-way fishing; taking turns to have a spell at the oars, while the other handles the rod.

The oarsman need never feel deprived. Handling the boat and scanning the water is just as exciting as doing the fishing – watching for a rise, or the glint of a flank underwater; taking a cross-reference on the distant banks to pinpoint the lie; holding the boat steady, or edging it a yard or two this way or that to help the angler according to the wind. It is indeed a combined effort – each angler contributing equally to the result.

It is enormous fun. Putting out a fairly short line to start with, then quickly working stripped line through the rings and rolling out a long loop; mended, repeated and mended again; until a big "wheel" has been formed – round which, if carefully drawn, the line will travel (pulled through the "little hands") guiding the flies in all sorts of directions according to the angles thrown. Sometimes working them directly away from the boat.

To induce our flies to wander about all over the place without our having to re-cast is very exciting. Quite irrespective of the results, it offers a new-found pleasure: yet another example of there being so much more to angling than the catching of fish. And the more skill we acquire, the greater the fun. Until, at length, it becomes a sport or even an art form, in its own right. It teaches us a profound lesson: that there is always something new to be thought about in angling; something original to be done.

It is a salutary reminder that we don't know everything there is to be known about either casting a fly or fishing it.

But it can be very tiring, both at the oars and with the rod, for the action is, literally, non-stop. Often it is with relief that one changes places – so as to use a different set of muscles.

And interspersed with sessions of two-way control, one can cover so much water all round a big arc broadside on to the boat, downwind and across wind, using the various methods of (mainly) roll and double Speycasting.

Never do the flies come back over the boat. Always, they are in view, out in front of you. Confident of his safety, whoever is at the oars can relax. Never again need lurk that fear of old – a fly in his ear, or worse. Metaphorically, he can take off his hat and turn his collar down.

The overhead cast!

The roll cast. Weight taken on the right leg as before.

Angler perfectly relaxed. Body
unmoving. All the work being done
with arm and wrist only.

On the river. *Rollcasting straight back downstream*. Line is drawn in and held taut with the left hand as the rod is raised at the start of the cast. When the "key" position is reached, sufficient loop will have formed to "kiss the water" preparatory to making the forward stroke, thus controlling the speed of the loop by means of the "little hands" as it unrolls.

And away it goes, shooting out above the water, taking all the slack line with it.

Finish of the reverse roll cast. Note
the angler's relaxed stance, there is
no body waggling or shoulder
rolling. Spare line is shot as rod
returns to horizontal and the
cast curls out above the water.

In the power stroke of the single-
handed reverse roll cast, cut the
hand to the right with a
"Screwdriver" twist – just as we
should do with the left hand in
reverse double-handed fishing –
except that now it is not the
fingernails but the back of the
hand that finishes up pointing at
the sky.

Forward stroke, punching the line
out with a powerful elliptical curve
aimed slightly upwards to ensure a
delicate touchdown.

*Reverse roll cast*, shot from the open side.

Up in the perfect "key" position. Line held taut with left hand. It is essential that this hand is not allowed to wander – if it does the cast will collapse.
*Note*: It is only feasible to reverse roll cast from the left bank if the line can be kept clear of obstructions. It is much more of a cast of the right bank.

*Double Spey cast*, as from the right

… exactly the same pattern of rod movement as used with the double-handed rod. Brought upstream to the left, taking care not to let it stray too high, then back again downstream to the right – having described a shallow figure-of-eight …

... following the curve of a new moon, up goes the rod into a re-directed roll cast ...

As line, leader and fly unfold at the finish of the power stroke, we notice that the angler has remained stationary throughout. Nothing has been allowed to diminish the spring of the rod.

By the way, when using a single-handed rod, hold the cork grip close to the reel. When playing a large fish I hold it at the top end, or even several inches above, with the butt braced either against my forearm or my chest.

... and aimed well above its touchdown point the fly is punched out towards its new destination ...

The man who thought Speycasting
was sissy.

*Reverse double Spey cast*, as from the left bank.

The rod is brought up to the right ...

... switched back to the left ...

225

... then brought up to the reverse "key" position the right hand straight above the head ...

... the all-important loop forms on the angler's left hand side with sufficient line controlled by the surface tension for the cast to be made without line "crack".

Now the loop is punched out and the line released by the left hand. It is at this crucial moment of the power stroke that the angler must resist any temptation to bend his body forward or *push* with the rod. Reverse casting can be very powerful provided the rod is allowed to do the work. Pushing the rod away with the right hand is a common fault.

But here the rod has done its job and the line goes whizzing out over the water.

*A hundred years ago*

An extra long line can be made in the following manner: Get out as much line as you can by making the steeple cast, then pull about 2 yds. of line off the reel, hold the rod in the right hand, and the loose line about a yard from the first ring in the left hand. Then cast, and just before you check the rod at the end of the forward cast, let go the line which you hold in your left hand. The spare line will then, if you manage well, shoot out through the rings. Before making the second cast, this extra line must be gathered in. This method is one which I frequently practise myself, not only because it enables me to get out a long line, but because the fly never falls lighter than when the line is shot out in the manner described.

John Bickerdyke

Various poses in *the single Spey cast* ...

... swinging to the right and bringing the line upstream ...

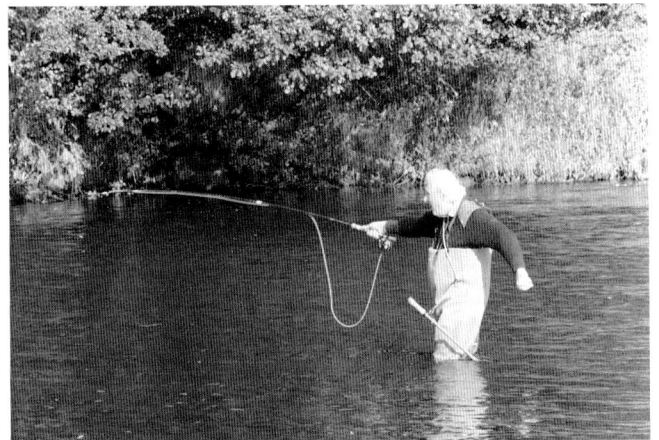

... well clear of the rod and about forty-five degrees above the right shoulder ...

... plenty of room; plenty of time to make the forward stroke, and when the rod comes down ...

... slack line shoots out as the line straightens over the water.

*Reverse single Spey cast.* With a reverse figure-of-eight lift-off, the fly has been brought up to the angler's left and placed out on the water at an angle of about forty-five degrees upstream. During this manoeuvre the angler has swung slightly from his hips to the left, keeping his right arm straight. A big loop of line has formed and to finish off he has only to make a reverse roll cast in the desired direction.

The forward stroke. As with the double-handed rod, I find I can make a more powerful cast with the right wrist in reverse than by changing hands and using the left wrist.

"The angler, having acquired some proficiency in casting from his right side, should next practise casting from his left side, still holding his rod in his right hand ..."

John Bickerdyke, *The Book of the All-Round Angler* (qv)

An interesting reference to a *reverse* cast. Exactly how he made it is not clear, but his excellent advice seems not to have been widely followed at the time.

Great controversy rages in the smoking-rooms of fishing inns as to whether you should or should not wear a strap round your waist when wading in dangerous waters. Many anglers assert that if you do use a belt, and do not allow the water to get freely into your waders, if you should have to swim for your life the buoyancy of your legs will drown you by causing your head to go under water and your feet to bob about on the surface like corks. I have even met men who vowed that they had seen this happen. Well, that is all utter nonsense. A salmon fisher who has been swept away by the stream may be stunned or numbed by having his head or his limbs struck hard against a boulder, or he may be dazed by the knocking about that he gets when he is trying to struggle to his feet in a swift current that is tumbling him along down the stream, but he has no need to fear the result of having air in his waders. His feet will not bob about on the surface or sink his head. I have tried it more than once by deliberately upsetting out of a boat when crossing the river in my waders, and the result is nothing of the sort. The buoyancy is enough to keep your legs well up, but it does not bother you at all, and you swim quite easily.

A. H. Chaytor, *Letters to a Salmon Fisher's Sons* 1910

# XVI WATER SAFETY

THE ABILITY to wade, and wade deep where acceptable, is an asset to every Speycaster since, by comparison with fishing from a high bank, punching out a loop is such a simple matter – our being closer to the surface making it easier for the "little hands" to control the line.

But rivers vary enormously. Some have evenly-gravelled runs and glides which are easily waded. Others, awkward and treacherous, have slimy rocks with deep, sullen pools, where a single false step may take the unsuspecting non-swimmer straight over a sunken ledge – into eternity.

On the river, wading is the most common cause of fishing accidents, and it is probable that breast waders are involved in the majority of these. No criticism of breast waders is intended. The point is simply that the higher your waders, the deeper you are tempted to wade – until one day a step too many is taken. When this happens, the water is not up to your knees or thighs, but your chest, and you find yourself being swept off your feet into deep water.

Mistakes are easily made. Places quite safe to wade when the river is, say, a foot above summer level, may be very difficult after a further rise of two inches. In a lake, a two-inch rise means that your safe wading depth is reduced by exactly that amount. Two extra inches in the river mean not only two inches of extra depth, but a stronger current. This added pressure increases the water level against your back or side. It also causes you to lean over at a greater angle against the currrent – thus further reducing the safety margin of your waders. The combination of these two factors results in a loss of considerably more than two inches.

When wading for any distance downstream, always be sure of the depth of water between the bank and wherever you happen to be. Your path may be along an underwater ridge with deep water on either side, in which case the only retreat is straight back upstream. Wading against even a weak current is a great deal more difficult than wading with it. Your return will be made even more difficult if, while you have been fishing, the river has begun to rise.

Such a rise may be entirely unexpected. It is not by any means unusual for a downpour further up the valley to affect the river, although not a drop of rain has fallen in your locality. Or perhaps there has been a release of water from an up-river dam. The early stages of such a rise are not immediately evident to anyone intent on fishing. The water level may creep up unnoticed – until the margin of safety is passed.

Most fishing accidents result in little more than a wetting. An angler gets his or her boots full, or stumbles and falls in shallow water. But season after season comes news of fatalities. Someone has lost his balance or been swept away when wading; a loose rock has toppled over; a piece of river bank has collapsed; a boat has capsized ... people have drowned. Accidents such as these can happen very suddenly; indeed they usually do. Within seconds of being safe and relaxed, the unlucky man finds himself floundering out of his depth. Terrified, he throws up his arms and screams.

Two involuntary actions. Both fatal.

Many lives would be spared if people would only think *beforehand* of the correct action to take in the event of emergency.

It is the unexpectedness of most accidents that carries the greatest threat to safety: the shock of a sudden plunge into cold water, followed immediately by panic — panic caused by the thought of being heavily clothed and shod, and out of one's depth. It has been said — and a surprising number of people believe it — that if a fisherman wearing waders falls into deep water, his boots will drag him down.

They will do nothing of the sort.

It is a perfectly simple matter to swim fully clothed and wearing any sort of waders. Their weight when submerged is negligible, and although they make swimming no easier they certainly don't make it impossible.

It has been claimed in the angling press that air trapped in breast waders will turn you upside-down, stick your arse up and push your head under.

What nonsense.

Even sillier, it has been suggested more than once that to prevent this happening, an angler should carry a "sharp instrument" so that "if he falls in and air is trapped in his waders, forcing his legs up, he can puncture or cut them to release it immediately".

This is not only nonsense but dangerous nonsense. In the whole of a long sporting life, I can remember nothing quite so stupid.

To argue with people as foolish as this is unproductive. I can only treat such advice with the derision it deserves. And I advise my readers to do likewise, because if you don't, if you are silly enough to try slashing away when floundering out of your depth, you will assuredly drown.

As quoted at the start of this chapter, the idea that air in your waders could drown you was explored by A. H. Chaytor over eighty years ago. And from a lifetime's experience of swimming in all seasons heavily booted and wearing all sorts of clothes when fishing, sailing and wildfowling, I can fully endorse what he wrote.

It is not *air* that drowns most people, it is *panic*. Air will save you, if you only give yourselves a chance. When you are seized with panic, rational thought vanishes. Fear locks the mind as it locks the muscles. Apart from suffering a heart attack or cramp, most people found drowned, face down, died because, panic-stricken, they were unable to make any sensible move to save themselves. There are many examples of people drowning in a depth of only three or four feet. A sudden and unexpected fall into the clutch of icy water induced a state of utter shock, so that panic-stricken they were unable to stand up – which was all they had to do. Instead, they lay there and died.

Panic can be avoided by mental preparation: by thinking about it all before it happens. Then, provided you can swim, no acute sense of alarm need accompany most of your tumbles into deep water – whether in river, loch or sea. In fact, to retain the grip on your rod presents no great problem. I have done this many times on various rivers when bankside conditions made it impossible otherwise to follow a big fish downstream. (Most recently was on the River Tweed, when a thirty-five pounder took me down through the middle arch of Norham Bridge. Wading the spit above and unable to check the fish – but determined not to be broken – I simply stepped into deep water, lay on my back in the stream, and drifted down in pursuit. After clearing the bridge I paddled myself to the side one-handed and landed the fish in some slack water sixty yards below. No story in it.)

In order to enjoy such a feeling of security you should practise paddling about fully clothed and booted one warm summer afternoon, paying particular attention to the backstroke. Most emergency swimming should be carried out on the back. There is nothing in the least difficult about it. On the contrary you will probably be surprised to find how easy it is. And it is very, very important, for it will arm you with confidence. Apart from considering the possibility of heart failure or cramp (and cramp, at least, can be provided against: a bottle of Quinine-Sulphate tablets lives in my tackle-bag) the thought of falling into deep water will no longer be one of fear.

When the worst happens – perhaps an undermined river bank collapses; a boat capsizes, or a shingle bottom slides away beneath your feet – and you suddenly find yourself plunging fully clothed, rod in hand, into the deeps – *don't* open your mouth and shout. Pay no attention to those old stories of drowning men coming up three times. If you ship enough water first time down, you won't come up at all. So – *keep your mouth shut.*

Provided you don't wave your arms about above your head you will soon bob up again. A fully-clothed living body is very buoyant. Even if you can't swim, there will be sufficient air trapped in your waders and various garments to keep you afloat for several minutes if you will only lie on your back.

If you can't manage to swim and hold the rod as well, drop it at once. Stretch your arms out in the "crucifix" position, let your legs come to the surface and keep your head lying well back in the water. Once in this position you can start shouting for help.

If in a river, don't try to swim against the current. Let yourself drift downstream, feet first, then it will be your boots that strike a rock, not your head. Paddle away meanwhile with your hands and edge in towards the bank.

But the most important advice I can give you is to *work out in advance* what to do in case of emergency. Study the following pictures and think about what *you* will do in a similar situation.

It may save your life.


## SOME THOUGHTS ON THE BOWLINE

On a cold winter afternoon a few years ago, four people fell into the water near a seaside esplanade while attempting to rescue a dog. Ropes thrown to them proved useless. One by one they grasped a rope's end and were dragged almost to the top of the sloping embankment, only to fall back again into the sea as the rope ends pulled through their fingers. All four were drowned. It is a horrifying story, because I have not the slightest doubt that if bowlines had been tied in the ends of those ropes no lives would have been lost.

It is not likely that you will find a coil of rope handy on a river bank when someone falls in. But in case of emergency you can at least take some sort of positive action – even if you don't plunge in and drag him out. Quickly cut off leader and fly, tie a generous bowline in the end of your flyline and cast it to him. If he can only get his hand through the loop and hold it as shown on p.250 there is every chance he can be swung round into shallow water. I first tried this out many years ago when practising life-saving methods on the river, and it worked well. Later, some friends used it successfully on the Dee. (For other notes on water safety, see *Falkus and Buller's Freshwater Fishing*, revised edition, 1988. Also my film *Salmo the Leaper*, now available on video.)

> *Note*: On a well appointed fishery a coil of rope with bowline ready tied should be hanging up on every beat. Preferably on every pool, from start to finish of the day's fishing.

It must of course be understood that no bowline is going to save you if you panic, a definition of which will be found on p.244. In the meantime the following pictures will I trust help to dispel the recent hysterical clamour of the "wader-slashers".

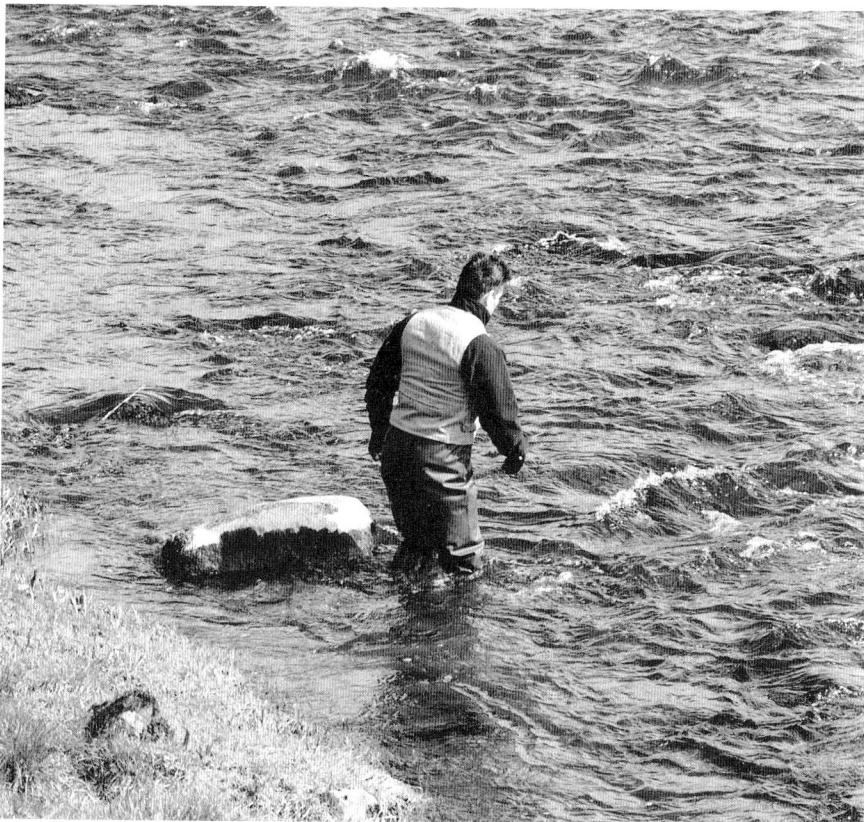

Fully clothed and wadered, Neil Barcock of Cockermouth (a former pupil and now a highly accomplished teacher of my Speycasting technique) walks along an underwater ledge into a deep, turbulent salmon pool. Irritated beyond measure by much of the nonsense printed in the angling press, he has volunteered to demonstrate some of the principles of water safety I have been preaching for many years.

Nearly at the place where a wading angler might make a false move, he glances back to confirm that the cameraman is ready.

Then steps off into deep water.

Immediately, the angle of the current drags him out into the middle of the river. It is this panic-inducing moment that leads to so many fatalities.

But as he is whisked downstream, perfectly prepared for what is happening, Barcock turns on his back, stretches his arms out and kicks with his legs.

Aided by the air trapped in his waders, his feet come to the surface. From this point on he is perfectly safe.

*Note*: Once you are in this "crucifix" position, legs up, arms outstretched, you can float safely down the length of any pool – paddling with your hands towards the bank until a suitable landing place is reached where you can crawl out.

If at any time – particularly at the moment of falling in – you throw up your arms and shout for help …

… you will sink.

And if you happen to suck in enough water, you will stay sunk. But if you don't lose your head, just keep your mouth shut and lower your arms, you will soon …

... bob up again, none the worse for going under.

Now lie on your back. Arms out. Mouth well clear of the water.

This is the life-saver: the classic "safe" position. At this point you can start calling for help.

Over the years a great deal of rubbish has been printed about the danger of having air trapped in breast waders. It is supposed to lift your legs up and push your head under: to roll you over and lift your bum, so that your head gets thrust face-downwards – hence the ridiculous notion of "slashing your wader legs with a sharp instrument"! To expose the fatuity of this, Neil Barcock rolls over on his belly and ...

... strikes out for the bank with a powerful breast stroke.

Without the slightest difficulty he plunges to the side, purposely choosing a place where the bank shelves gently.

*Note*: When in shallow water, *don't* try to stand up and walk. Waders full of water will soon exhaust you. Stay on hands and knees and ...

... crawl out.

Then, before taking any steps, drain the water from your waders. After that, some dry clothes (from the duffle bag stored in your car for every fishing trip) will soon see you back in action. *Don't forget*: in addition to a change of clothes, always pack a spare pair of waders. A rest, a nip of Scotch and you will be raring to go, feeling none the worse for your brief adventure.

Most falls into deep water need prove no more serious than this – provided you keep your head. *It is panic that drowns most people.* (For a definition of panic, see below.)

## PANIC

Panic can be defined as acute, overwhelming *fear or anxiety* in which the regulatory mechanisms for controlling this anxiety are lost. Inherent in the definition is the lack of purpose and lack of any logical thought to control one's actions during a state of panic. The dividing line between anxiety, fear, terror and panic is probably at the point where logic and purposeful behaviour is lost.

Simple anxiety has a physiological purpose. It is mediated by special nerves, namely the sympathetic system, and has as its purpose the ability to alert the animal or individual for, as the great Sherrington said, fight or flight. Indeed, as simple anxiety increases, so does the standard of performance, this being due to the fact that the brain, i.e., the hypothalamus in the brain has alerted the pituitary to produce hormones which in turn cause the adrenal gland to pour out steroids. On top of this the sympathetic system stimulates the production of nonadrenalin and the heart increases in rate, respiration increases in rate, sugar is increased and the body, generally, is prepared for action.

Mild degrees of anxiety increase learning and performance, as every actor will know. However, once the anxiety acutely reaches a point where panic sets in, there is extreme fear which abrogates logical thought and reasoning and increases breathlessness, palpitations, dizziness and fatigue. The muscles burn up glucose and convert it to lactate, the person hyperventilates and all of this increased metabolism is deleterious to any purposeful (physiological) action.

It can be clearly seen therefore that a person falling into the water or having to maintain logical thought and purposeful action under conditions of panic would be totally unable to do so. Indeed, actions that occur are likely to be counterproductive, non-purposeful.

I would suspect that panic is responsible for many deaths in many situations where, if the individual could only have maintained a normal anxiety and normal reasoning, the life would have been saved by purposeful action.

(For this definition of panic I am indebted to my old friend Peter O. Behan. Professor of Neurology, Glasgow.)

245

This sequence has been produced to prove how simple it is to swim down a pool holding one's rod and paddling to the side one-handed without any undue effort, although the water is deep and very cold (the photographs were taken in early April).

Playing the part of an angler fishing down the pool, Neil Barcock wades along an underwater ledge preparatory to his immersion...

... then as he approaches the deepest part of the pool, at an arranged signal he steps off into the main channel ...

... nine feet of strong, swirling current, which quickly ...

... sets him at an angle across the river towards the opposite bank.

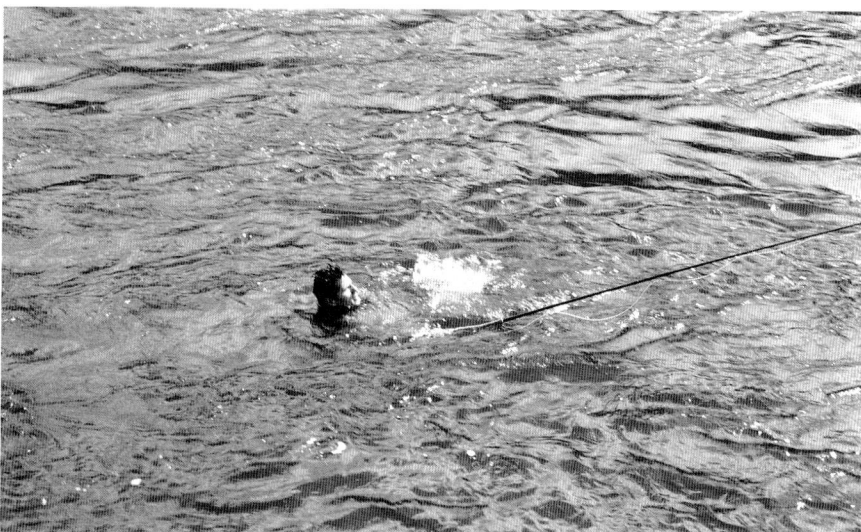

Lying on his back facing downstream, keeping his rod up with one hand, paddling with the other and kicking with his legs, he edges back towards his own bank ...

... making short work of finding his way into shallowing water,

As soon as he drops a foot and touches bottom he plunges forward ...

... throws his rod up on the bank clear of his exit from the water, and crawls out.

Kneeling for the camera to show his total unconcern before lying back and draining his waders.

## Importance of the Bowline

Never throw a rope to anyone in distress without tying a bowline in the end of it. A bowline is a life-saver, a loop that will not slip. To anyone with cold fingers a plain rope's end is virtually useless. A bowline transforms a rope into a life preserver of the greatest importance. If at present you are unable to tie the knot, practise doing so at once until you can make it blindfolded. Accidents can happen in the dark as well as daylight.

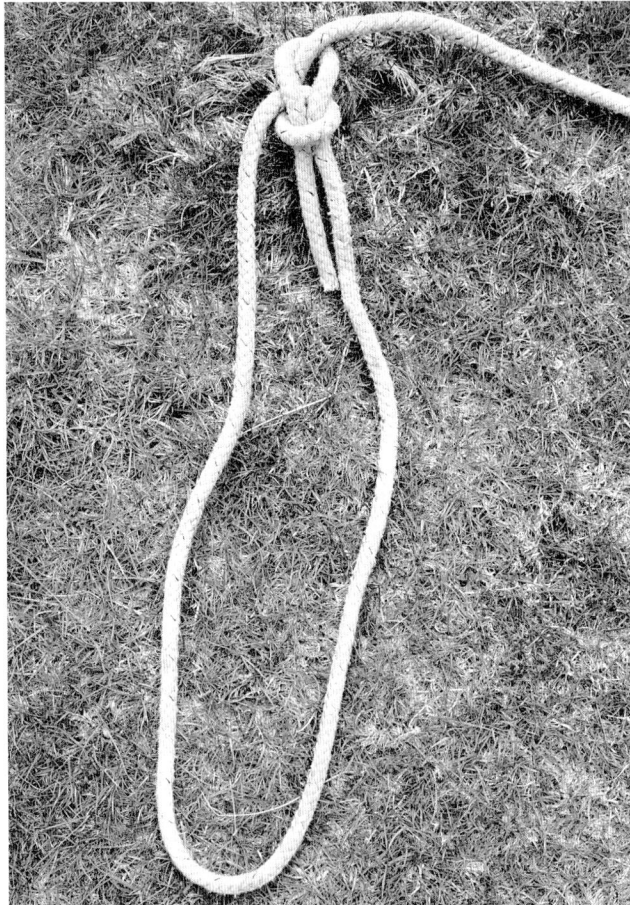

The bowline is a knot that will not slip and allow the loop to crunch your hand. Safest of all is the loop large enough to slip over head and shoulders. But even when hand-held, the loop is incomparably better than a plain end.

A better way to hold the loop is by slipping a hand through, holding both sides together (as shown) and letting the loop pull tight round the wrist. This grip is a life-saver.

# TAILPIECE

At this point I hear a plaintive voice crying: "What about safety-jackets, aren't they being worn quite extensively these days?"

Yes, I believe they are. Indeed, I am told that on some waters their use is compulsory. But, never having worn or even seen one, I can offer no guidance as to which, if any, is the most sensible.

I am tempted to observe that this new form of regulation smacks strongly of the "nanny" state that threatens to smother us today – all so distant from the country I was brought up in. Instead of acquiring a sense of self-confidence by being taught about swimming and the ways of wind and water (which was all part of my education), the poor buggers find themselves clapped haplessly into compulsory water-wings.

In fairness to safety aids I must emphasize that, from his own experience, my old friend Fred Buller speaks highly of an inflatable waistcoat marketed by one of our well-known tackle manufacturers. This model expands automatically on coming into contact with water. It sounds thoroughly practical, and if it saves your life there is an end to the matter.

But I offer one word of advice: I have a feeling that if you rely implicitly on your safety-jacket and one day, through forgetfulness or some mischance, you suddenly suffer the unexpected shock of plunging into the deeps without your dummy, the immediate reaction of helplessness and despair may well engender panic, in which case you will quite needlessly drown.

Think about it. Wear all the safety-waistcoats you wish, but do, please do, "make assurance double sure": practise swimming fully clothed and booted. It will provide a new-found confidence.

After all, the technique illustrated in this chapter is so easy, and so safe. Remember, whatever happens, if you give yourself the opportunity to use them, you have some in-built water-wings which can never be mislaid and on which you can always rely. They are called lungs.

# INDEX